Making Wood Tables

Practical Projects for Every Room

Hugh Foster

Drawings by Malcolm Wells

 STERLING PUBLISHING CO., INC. NEW YORK

684.13

Dedication
For Malcolm Wells,
il miglior fabbro

Some of the material that appears in this book has been published in a different form in the following publications: *Popular Woodworking, Creative Woodworking & Crafts, Craftsman Tools at Home, Using the Skil 4355 Scrolling Jig Saw* and *WoodCarving.*

904323

Library of Congress Cataloging-in-Publication Data

Foster, Hugh.
    Making wood tables : projects for every room / Hugh Foster.
       p. cm.
    Includes index.
    ISBN 0-8069-8629-8
    1. Tables. 2. Furniture making.   I. Title.
  TT197.5.T3F67   1994
  684.1'3—dc20   93-44537
                                                CIP

10 9 8 7 6 5 4 3 2 1

Published by Sterling Publishing Company, Inc.
387 Park Avenue South, New York, N.Y. 10016
© 1994 by Hugh Foster
Distributed in Canada by Sterling Publishing
% Canadian Manda Group, P.O. Box 920, Station U
Toronto, Ontario, Canada M8Z 5P9
Distributed in Great Britain and Europe by Cassell PLC
Villiers House, 41/47 Strand, London WC2N 5JE, England
Distributed in Australia by Capricorn Link (Australia) Pty Ltd.
P.O. Box 6651, Baulkham Hills, Business Centre, NSW 2153, Australia
Manufactured in the United States of America

Sterling ISBN 0-8069-8629-8

Contents

Acknowledgments

A hearty thanks to the following people: Mac Wells (architect at the Underground Gallery, 673 Satucket Road, Brewster, Massachusetts 02631), for his drawings, without which this book wouldn't be half as useful as it is; Gene Bauch, for demonstrating door lamination and providing understandable technical advice; Bob Ayers, for the fabulous *Ducks Unlimited* table; Peter Mader, for a pair of tables included in this book; Matt Swadner, for laying tile on a moment's notice when my photographer helper vanished; Dr. H. B. "Ding" Roholt, for sharing the lovely pine burl tables with us; Carlo Venditto, president of CMT Tools, for supplying router bits which have been used to make some of these tables more interesting; Jason Betz, for a few of the photos that appear in this book; Elizabeth Foster, my wife, for many of the photos that include the author, and for much, much more; and, last but not least, the folks at Sterling—for waiting for the manuscript.

Introduction

It seems that almost every serious project a woodworker builds is either a chest, a chair, or some kind of table. In most ways, the table is by far the simplest of these because it is basically a flat surface of wood or other material mounted at some height from the floor. Yet, there are as many varieties of table as there are uses for them.

This book includes mostly simple tables for novice and intermediate woodworkers and for those who want to build tables the correct way rather than take on complicated projects. Tables don't have to be complicated to make to be attractive. Over the couple of years I've been working on this book, I've seen many designer tables that looked absolutely useless. Balanced on tripods, held up by four cast-concrete rabbets, painted with luminous fish scales, etc., many of these avant-garde tables are not the type of table most woodworkers would build. Such tables are not featured here. By the time you have read this book and built one or two of the tables presented, you'll be firmly enough grounded in the fundamentals of tablemaking that you'll be able to design and build your own avant-garde tables—if you want them.

What this book does is show how to build with relatively few tools and novice-level skills good, sturdy tables for every room of the home. There are some tables here that have virtually *no* joints—and require virtually *no* tools. All the tables are straightforward to build.

There are many advantages to making your own tables. One is the money saved. Every time I walk into a furniture store, I am shocked by the comparatively high prices of even simple furniture. Of course, these prices have to reflect the material, labor, space, and transportation costs of both making and selling the furniture; considering all that, it's little wonder that commercial furniture is expensive. Hobbyist woodworkers with even very modest shops and fairly minimal equipment might save enough by building their own tables to justify adding a piece of equipment or two or a stack of interesting wood to their shops.

While many woodworkers prefer to buy rough-sawn timbers and joint and plane their own boards, it is perfectly possible to build attractive projects without doing this. Materials from the lumberyard or building center can be perfectly satisfactory, and all the projects shown in this book have been built with such material. My small town lumberyard offers several species of softwood (pine, fir, spruce) and several species of hardwood (Philippine mahogany, redwood, oak, and birch). Additionally, it has rather expensive glued-up panels of real mahogany, cherry, and walnut.

A stack of bird's-eye maple cost $220 in mid-1992, less than any one of the four or five commercial tables made from it would have cost—assuming that you could buy tables made of wood of this quality. And these tables made of bird's-eye maple will be made of *real* wood rather than a fancy veneer over a core. Plywood and veneers have their place in furniture-making, to be sure, but most home woodworkers will build little enough furniture that they can afford to use solid material. Veneering is difficult enough to be useful only when working with the rarest of woods. Most ordinary plywood simply isn't pretty enough to bother with, and most of it isn't really very inexpensive.

Money isn't the only reason to build your own tables. Indeed, if you do follow my suggestions and buy a new piece of equipment or two, you're certain to find that you won't come out ahead economically, at least not right away. In my shop, I've concentrated on making furniture for my own home rather than to derive a small income from making the occasional piece for other people. This recreational value can't be stressed too highly. I enjoy woodworking at least as much as nearly anything I do.

While commercial furniture is built to serve general needs or to look good, your furniture can be made to fit your particular needs. Two examples illustrate this principle: First, end tables should be equal in height to the arm of the piece of furniture next to them. This isn't the way commercial furniture is made, but such concerns are specifically addressed for the end tables in this book. Second, you will notice that most commercial workbenches are far too low. The highest one I know of is only 33½″ high; most are 30–32″. When I built my first workbench, it was also too low; I added blocks to the bottom until it was the height I felt served me best: 39″. This is 5½″ higher than the highest commercial bench. At 5′11″, I'm not excessively tall. The 39″ height is about 4″ below my elbows, a height I can work at without stooping over the work nearly all the time. On those rare occasions when I work with very

thick stock, I use a low stool as I work at the bench, or I spread the work out on some 30″ high sawhorses.

The real message of this last example is simple: The plans for the tables in this book are intended as guidelines. Think before you begin cutting your stock; make the project fit your circumstances, just as I have made these projects fit mine. That way, you'll end up with a houseful of tables that you and your family will be proud to use. When you achieve this, you will have helped me realize my goals.

A photograph and a drawing of the table are included for virtually all of the projects presented in this book. So are parts lists. There are a few tables such as the pine burl table which are included to demonstrate intriquing design possibilities, and as such do not have cutting lists or drawings. None of the projects is truly difficult; the most difficult project here could be classified at an "intermediate" level. A hurried woodworker, however, might find some of the projects to be troublesome. The key to overcoming the difficulty of many projects is to simply slow down. Impatience destroys more woodworking projects than lack of skill. Patient people are usually the most skillful.

I-1. This computer desk is just one of the many tables you will learn to build in the following pages.

Table-Making Information

1.
Safety Techniques

Woodworking is a potentially dangerous activity. Cutters are sharp, and high-power motors can move them at very fast speeds. Shop accidents may have a number of different causes which include (but are not limited to) operator error (which includes carelessness and haste) and equipment failure. I know from personal experience that a serious shop accident can take a very long time to heal. In most cases, the operator is often the chief cause of the accident. Yet, other woodworkers have told me stories that suggest that in *some* cases equipment makers are also to blame for the accident, even when the accident is not directly the fault of the machinery.

Woodworking machines are designed with safety in mind. If you use your tools in the way they were intended, you minimize the possibility of being hurt by them. If you follow these safety procedures, you will ensure a safer working environment:

1. Use all the safety equipment on your tools. This includes the guards. You will notice that in most of the photos in this book that show a table saw being used, the saw appears to have no blade guard. The blade guard was removed to get a clear illustration. Make sure you use your guards.

2. Keep your cutters sharp and maintain them properly. Dull tools force you to exert extra pressure when you cut. This makes you more likely to slip and, thereby, get your hands in the way of the cutting edge.

3. Always wear safety glasses or goggles. When using a tool that throws lots of chips, wear a face shield as well. When using a loud tool, wear hearing protection. Wear a dust mask whenever you're sanding or doing operations that produce lots of dust. If there is a dust collector available for a tool, use it *every time you switch on the tool.*

4. Wear steel-tipped shoes when you are woodworking. Don't wear loose clothing. Roll up your sleeves. If you have long hair, tie it back. Anything loose can be pulled into a cutter if it gets caught. Don't wear jewelry, not even a ring.

5. Do not do any woodworking if you have taken drugs or alcohol. Even over-the-counter and prescription drugs can cause drowsiness and other effects that would make it dangerous to use woodworking tools, so read the labels and follow your doctor's advice.

6. Most important, pay attention to what you're doing. Let your good sense be your guide. Think through each procedure before you do it. If you feel it presents a safety hazard, find an alternative procedure.

Remember, it's important to think about safety on a regular, ongoing basis. Only your constant vigilance will protect you from injury in the woodworking shop.

2.
Workshop Tools and Equipment

How big a shop and what kinds of tools and equipment are needed to build the projects in this book? When I was a younger woodworker, I skipped many desirable projects because I didn't have all the tools the project's designers described. I probably still don't have them, but I know fellow woodworkers who will let me use theirs. For instance, practically *no* woodworker can afford to buy a 30″ surface planer, but it shouldn't be hard to rent a planer and its operator at a small millwork company for approximately $25–$35/hour. Though this may sound expensive, it represents only about 1/1,000 the purchase price of such a tool; besides, the pro will plane the material for you far faster than you might do alone, so savings in time might make this planing very cost-effective.

You will probably need far less shop than you think you do. I built my very first projects by first composing cutting lists (usually drawn up by someone else), which I brought to the lumberyard where, for an additional charge, they did the cutting. I built the project at home with just a few hand tools.

You don't really *need* as many tools as you probably want. If you are thinking about buying a tool, first borrow it from someone to use once. This way, you will be able to determine if you will need to use it again and if it is the brand you want. If it's a tool that you suspect you'll use only once or twice in your woodworking career, rent it next time you need it.

Now that tools are quite expensive, shop carefully, buy the best tools for the job when shopping for new tools, but buy secondhand tools as often as possible. Unfortunately, like most woodworkers, I have bought tools on impulse, and have been influenced by style, price, availability, or, worse, a smooth-talking salesman. Being a good bit wiser now than I was when I began my woodworking "career," I feel qualified to make some observations about the errors we make when we buy tools, and some suggestions about how we should buy them.

My first tool, bought in the late 1960s, was a 9″ radial arm saw. I was 23, and I couldn't drive a nail, but I had bought a house that needed a lot of work—it was all a young teacher could afford—and I learned woodworking through trial and error. We used the saw a lot as we remodelled. That saw generated my interest in woodworking.

The radial saw was great for cutoffs, but it never did live up to the expectations I had for it. It could be made to do at least most of the things described in woodworking books, but not by one so impatient as I. The best use for the radial arm saw is making precisely square cutoffs. Set up the machine to do that, and leave it in place to do that only, and you'll love it.

Ripping on a radial arm saw is neither particularly safe nor particularly accurate, so I bought a motorized table saw for a few hundred dollars. For several years it was fine for ripping and other activities. However, because it didn't have sufficient power to rip 2″-thick hard maple for whole

Illus. 2-1. A table saw is an important workshop power tool. This table saw is being used with a shop-made tenoning jig to cut tenons.

afternoons at a time, we eventually had to get another tool. When the opportunity to pick up a powerful—and more accurate—UniSaw® table saw arrived, I grabbed it. I soon got a surprise, however: It cost well over $100 for the supplies to run 240 volts into my shop. Certainly power is as much an element in this sort of decision as is the kind of work.

Over a dozen or more years of use, the UniSaw still performs well, but I now expect even more from it and the other tools in the workshop. For instance, the biscuit joiner has made it possible to join a mitred carcass very strongly, but I cannot cut the joint accurately or quickly enough on my UniSaw to be able to join it together efficiently with biscuits. Is it time for yet another table saw? Since I surely cannot afford a new saw, I will have to work towards achieving that sort of precision with the machines at hand and some of the new table-saw accessories.

My next tool was a 6″ jointer with a medium-length bed. It served me well for ten years; a jointer is a necessity in a shop, probably one of the two essential stationary tools. The longer the bed, the flatter the cuts it will take. A surface planer is equally handy, and in Manitowoc, Wisconsin, the going rental rate is $25 per hour.

In the late 1970s I was doing even more shop work, and I was paying $2 an hour so I could stand in line to use the loudest, dullest, and oldest surface planer in America. (The "Columbus" inscription must have belonged to the fellow who brought it to America in 1492!) Complain as we did, those sessions were a bargain—but as it got more difficult to schedule a week's work around that Wednesday-night school session, I started to believe I needed my own planer.

There weren't really many affordable options. The planers that were available weren't wide or powerful enough or were of uneven quality. I did eventually attend several INCA seminars and meet countless dealers and users, and came to understand why there were so many avid INCA owners. The machines are powerful, accurately made, and capable of apparently unending first-class service in exchange for moderate care. As with most things, their expense is commensurate with their high quality. Today, one might reasonably choose the Makita 2012 or the Ryobi AP-10, which offer far more affordable options for 10–12″ planing.

My second drill press came from a garage sale. I spent hours modifying it, and it is far superior to the loose-quilled original I had bought from a major manufacturer. The jigs I have made for the drill have contributed more to its usefulness than the drill itself. If your requirements are for holes more than 8–10″ from the outside edge of a board, consider a radial drill press which, like a radial arm saw, is probably best adjusted to a single position and then left there. I once saw one of these very efficiently mounted from the ceiling rather than from the floor or a bench.

James Krenov, a woodworking author, wrote years ago that he'd rather have a good band saw than any other single saw. I read that remark with great skepticism, but now that I've seen some good band saws, I know he's right. Safer than the table saw for ripping and most other kinds of cuts, a powerful and well-tuned band saw can do nearly everything that a table saw can do. Buy the most powerful band saw and one with the deepest throat you can afford, and learn to operate it well. I scrapped my 10″ saw for a 14″ model, and that in turn for a 20″, 2 horsepower model.

My lathe, a decent enough machine, was purchased at a clearance sale. Underpowered and with insufficient speed variations, it was a trustworthy spindle-turning machine. For turning bowls, however, it left a great deal to be desired. Now I also own a Conover lathe with a variable-speed DC (direct-current) motor that makes it possible for me to do all sorts of turning—none of which is displayed in this book.

Thinking about my first lathes brings to mind the major fault of most "home" workshop equipment: They are underpowered by at least 50 percent. My band saw would likely be more satisfactory if its horsepower were roughly doubled. Had my 6″ jointer had ¾ or 1 hp instead of ½ hp, it would still be in my shop. I'd still have the motorized table saw had its motor been more powerful; we traded it in when we realized that we would destroy it if we continued to cut 2″ maple in the quantities we were cutting.

Setting up shop today is expensive. A shop with top-quality power tools and a minimal amount of hand tools and accessories will cost nearly as much as a new car. Many woodworkers who intend to build a few pieces of furniture for their own homes will have a hard time justifying this cost. With that thought in mind, how does one go about minimizing the cost of setting up shop? Here are some tips that will help you decide which tools to buy—and when to buy them:

1. *Consider how much table-making you intend to do.* Buy tools that reflect this. Realistic planning is important unless you are one of those rare folks for whom money is no object.

2. *Shop garage and estate sales and read the local "shopper" paper for tools.* You may want to consider placing a wanted ad there. It only costs a few dollars, and may work wonders. Try to arrange for "pre-sales," even if at premium cost. As someone who has sold tools this way, I can tell you that you'll be one of hundreds of callers for most tools, and it won't do you much good to try to negotiate the price. Each of the tools I sold went for more money than I paid for it, and each buyer got a bargain. My favorite hand tools have all come from garage or estate sales or "shopper" papers. For instance, I bought a handful of chisels for 50 cents that took me just a day to sharpen, temper, and add new handles to. Older hand tools may prove better than "newer" ones. Stanley has dropped its No. 40 chisels, and I believe there is nothing on the market that even begins to compare with these chisels for most hand woodworking.

3. *Consider the advantages of used tools:* I believe you'll be able to afford tools that are larger and heavier than those you'd be able to buy new and, at least when you're just starting out, you'll be able to have more of them.

4. *Buy the best-quality tool you can afford.* Not only are fine-quality tools a joy to work with, but it is cheaper to buy the right tool the first time than to destroy an inferior tool later on. Besides, you're less likely to get hurt with fine-quality tools.

5. *It is fair to borrow a tool once;* after that, buy it. If you don't need it enough to own it, you don't really need it! The tool makers of the world won't keep making fine-quality tools if we don't buy them.

6. Know how to inspect your purchases for wear and needed maintenance. If you have a lot of room in your workshop for older tools, and if you can keep them adjusted, these tools, by virtue of their weight and antivibration tendencies, might be a very wise investment.

7. Whether buying new or used tools, pay attention to their design. Is the tool designed simply enough that you will be able to repair it when it breaks? And if you can fix it, will you be able to get the parts?

8. Consider using three-cycle electrical power. If you do, you can obtain industrial-duty tools at hobby-shop prices.

9. Take the woodworking classes at your local school. They are usually inexpensive. The shops will be well-equipped with a variety of tools; sample them. Learn what you like and don't like. You may discover sources of tools and learn about the various brands; this may help you to find a bargain and/or avoid poor-quality tools.

10. Visit shops of other woodworkers. Sample their equipment, if you can; insurance premiums being what they are, you may have to settle for their comments.

11. Visit your tool dealers. Apprise them of the prices advertised in woodworking magazines and ask whether they will negotiate a discounted price. What service will they provide to justify their higher price? My experiences with mail-order vendors has been that they are honest and reputable, providing fast delivery of items that can't be bought locally or at good prices.

A word of advice here: It isn't fair to use your local dealer's expertise and time and then buy the tools through mail order in order to save a couple of dollars. The local dealer, after all, doesn't get paid for his expertise until you buy his tool. If he **has** expertise, buying from him is probably worth the extra cost.

12. Be sure to get some comfortable "hear muffs" and wear them whenever you are in a shop where power equipment is running. Noise pollution is an underrated problem with all power tools, and far too many of the older woodworkers I know are to some degree deaf.

13. Don't buy any tool without trying it first.

14. Buy your hand tools first, or at least as you progress. There are two reasons for this: You do the finest of your work with hand tools, and they escalate faster in cost than power equipment.

Hand tools are safer than power tools and, for many jobs, are only slightly slower. Of course, combining muscle power with precision, coordination, etc., takes effort and practice. Here are some hand tools that have been particularly useful in my shop:

A. *Chisels, ⅛ through 1 inch, by eighths of an inch.* Buy good ones. A matched set would be preferable to a random assortment. I am very partial to my Stanley #40 chisels (with the metal-capped plastic handles) for rough work like chopping dovetails, and to some very old, very long, wood-handled ones I found at a garage sale practically free for finer work.

B. *A carver's mallet for striking chisels.* Using a hammer destroys chisels, and a mallet is also easier to use. I bought a mallet with a polyurethane sheath; it doesn't mar the chisels the way a regular metal hammer would, and it has outlasted half a dozen of the regular wooden mallets.

C. *A Stanley #92 rabbet plane.* Having this and a *Record #73 rabbet plane* would be especially nice.

D. *A Stanley #60.5 block plane* (with an adjustable mouth). In approximately two hours, you can tune this inexpensive "hardware store" plane into a precision instrument. I can't imagine working wood without mine and its companion, the #95, which is now, regrettably, a very expensive specialty shop item.

E. *A marking gauge.* A Marples 2154 marking gauge is a high-quality marking gauge.

F. *A Warrington-pattern 10-ounce hammer,* which is extremely useful. I have two, one twice the price of the other; they are virtually indistinguishable from one another. Let the buyer beware!

G. *Oval-handled screwdrivers.* Buy the smaller set of screwdrivers; they will save your hands from blistering many times. Some makers also have "crutch pattern" screwdrivers to match; if you ever need a lot of torque, these are the ones for you.

H. *Files.* Regular files can be found at your local hardware stores, but good wood rasps can only be found at a good woodworkers' supply house.

I. *Rulers,* ideally 12-, 24-, and 48-inch stainless steel rulers. The Veritas hook ruler is particularly nice.

J. *Clamps.* You can't have too many clamps. You should have at least several of each of the following clamps: pipe or bar clamps with pipes 3, 4, and 6 feet long; Jorgensen #3712 clamps or their equivalent; Jorgensen #3718 clamps or their equivalent; C-clamps; hand screws; and cam-action clamps. Take special care to keep the clamps clean. Remember to use pads. Pinch-dogs can also be used as a substitute for clamps in certain situations, for example, in panel-making, where, if you can cut the panels overlength, they can be a terrific moneysaver.

K. *A heavy-duty glue remover.* Glue destroys planer blades, and will cost you time or money.

L. *A sharpening system.* Try other people's until you find the kind you like and then buy one. I use a Japanese flat-rotation system and good honing stones. Right now, my Arkansas stones are too good to throw out, but when they go, I think they will be replaced with Japanese stones.

M. *A good workbench.* Commercial workbenches are expensive. It is less expensive to make one. I made mine for somewhere around $200, and the nearest comparable commercial bench costs around $800, and **none** of the commercial benches is configured for lefthanders! Chapter 11 contains information for building a good-quality workbench. One last thought about the workbench: shop-made wooden bench dogs are much easier on your planes than the metal ones that are much more expensive.

15. Though every project in this collection can be built with just hand tools, if you're after some power tools to speed certain processes, consider first buying a sabre saw with a variable orbit. A good drill and then a good sander (probably an inexpensive random-orbit model) should be your next picks. My choice for the first stationary tool would be a jointer, followed by a table saw. In any event, acquire your tools slowly enough to master each. Be sure to always work safely.

Illus. 2-2. It is less expensive to build a workbench than to buy one. In Chapter 11 I describe how to build the workbench shown here.

3.
Table-Making Quiz

In this chapter, I provide some questions every woodworker should consider before attempting to build any table. "Answers" are provided after each question. These answers reflect my opinions regarding what constitutes a well-built project. Other woodworkers may disagree. This disagreement may stem from a general philosophy regarding table making. Some builders believe that *every* project will have mistakes that only the builder will recognize, an idea I might agree with. There is a difference, however, between a minor mistake and sloppy work. All woodworkers should strive to build a table at their highest level of competence.

1. On a lampstand/plant stand or other small table, using top-quality rather than average material and applying good craftsman principles will raise the price by:
   A. a few dollars
   B. double to triple what it would normally cost
   Answer: *A.* As you work through the questions in this quiz, you'll note that there are some small problems with the table illustrated. Should they be corrected? Correcting these problems on a small project such as this will increase its cost slightly. However, if you're interested in leaving a legacy of excellent woodworking, you will want to improve the table.

2. True or False: All the handsome woods are tropical exotics from endangered rain forests.

Answer: *Of course not!* Every wood is handsome if used for the right project. We don't need to use timbers from the rain forests to complete wonderful projects. With that said, let me also add that I feel woodworkers who boycott exotic timbers are contributing to the problem in the rain forest. The real problem in the Amazon is slash-and-burn agriculture; by boycotting rain-forest timbers, and consequently reducing the value of such timber, we may well have sped the process. I suspect that our "symbolic" rejection of these materials has an effect other than the intended one.

3. True or False: The small planks shown in Illus. 3-1 are joined properly to prevent warping.
Answer: *True.* The grain should be alternated as the narrow pieces are joined for a top panel or other panel (Illus. 3-2).

4. Illus. 3-3 shows a close-up of the wide apron on a table. Would the table be more useful if it has a drawer or two in its apron?
Answer: This is really a question of taste, but my answer would be that most of us have too little space, so I'd add the drawer if at all possible. Most people, though, would apparently disagree with me, for traditionally such drawers have almost never been included in a small table like this.

5. Do you notice anything unusual about the apron on the table shown in Illus. 3-3?

Illus. 3-1. These small planks are joined properly, to prevent warping.

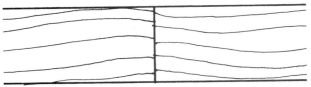

Illus. 3-2. Proper end-grain alignment for gluing. The object is to basically continue the existing curves.

Illus. 3-4 and 3-5. Note that the feet don't all meet on this flat surface, which is the machined top of a table saw.

Illus. 3-3. A wide apron. Note that the apron pieces are not tightly joined where they meet the left leg.

Illus. 3-5.

Answer: Two dissimilar pieces were used to make this apron piece, which is only about 8 or 9 inches long. There is no excuse for this.

6. The feet shown in Illus. 3-4 and 3-5 don't all meet on the flat surface. How do we correct this?

Answer: Make sure all the feet are square and, even before gluing, apply a leveler foot. Both these steps should always be done, for there are few things more annoying than small tables that tip over.

7. Do the legs in Illus. 3-6 and 3-7 look okay? Why or why not?

Answer: No. The legs are not "matched"—they have different grain orientations. One is glued up from two obviously different pieces. In a small project like this, it would add very little cost to use four like pieces for the legs—and it would take only an additional couple of minutes to align the grain orientation.

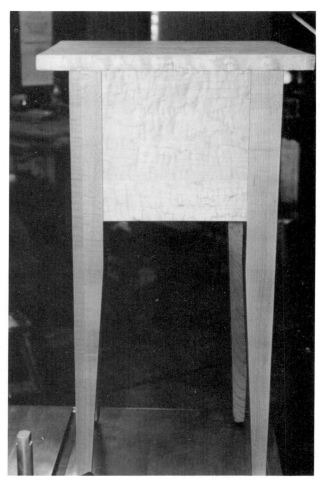

Illus. 3-7.

Illus. 3-6 and 3-7. The legs on these tables are not "matched."

8. Is the method shown in Illus. 3-8 the best way to attach a tabletop?

Answer: It depends. The table irons used are quick, dependable, not very expensive, and are not noticeable unless someone turns the table over to see how it's assembled. However, some table makers may consider these metal fasteners ugly and decide not to use them.

9. Is the tabletop in Illus. 3-9 handsome enough?

Answer: I'd like it better if the dark flecks in the bird's-eye appeared in diagonal rather than adjacent corners, but that's a real minor problem. Also, the glue line is quite visible although the

Illus. 3-8. Is this the best way to attach the top?

Illus. 3-9. The maple used on this top proves that exotic tropical hardwoods do not have to be used to create attractive tables.

joint is sufficiently well made. Maybe the table would look better if what are now its outside edges are joined. At any rate, it is handsome enough, and if the rest of the table were built to this standard the entire table would cost just about $50 to make. The out-of-pocket cost difference between this project and one that's absolutely perfect is about $20. This leads to the tenth and final question:

10. Can you afford not to do your best work?

Answer: The conclusion I hope you have reached is no. Hopefully, this quiz has given you something to think about. It may be true that the project shown in these examples is small and that some of the defects discussed are picayune, but excellence *is* within our grasp—all we really have to do is strive for it.

4.
Preparing Stock

Preparing stock is a part of every project that experienced woodworkers take for granted; woodworking authors haven't really treated stock preparation in quite a long time, and it is not being taught in woodworking classes. This is in stark contrast to what I learned in my junior high-school woodworking class in the late 1950s: We were given a rough-cut pine board and rudimentary instructions in the use of the hand saw and hand plane, and told we would be eligible to start making projects as soon as we created a 6″ x 6″ x ¾″ piece that was *perfectly* square and accurately sized in all dimensions. Many of us spent 13 or 14 *weeks* planing and cutting that board and many others like it. Not too proudly, I recall shedding approximately the board's weight in tears as I repeatedly failed this task. It's a wonder that my classmates and I ever became interested in woodworking.

While that junior high-school experience may have been excessive now that making square stock can so easily be done with today's power equipment, there's little reason not to begin each project with the advantages that square stock offers. As much as I hated preparing stock in the 1950s, it's now one of my favorite parts of a project. When I buy rough lumber, and that seems to be the only way to get fine woods without paying excessively high prices for them, I always enjoy surfacing it, just to see what beauties nature has left in store for me and/or for the user of the project. The pieces illustrated in this chapter—bird's-eye maple

and pecan—were prepared in two sessions. The results were beautiful stripes, great waves of grain, and some "wormy" sections which gave the finished project a look far more handsome than that associated with mass-produced furniture. All these "defects"—or beauty marks, as I prefer to call them—are surely a major contributor to the notion that custom-made furniture looks "more real" than does its mass-produced, commercial counterpart.

Another advantage of working with uniformly square stock is its convenience; professional woodworkers I know skim even commercial stock so that it's all the same thickness when they begin a project, rather than have to make adjustments when they glue-up panels. This is a worthwhile practice.

As with all table-making and woodworking operations, when working with square stock wear hearing protection and use dust-collection and/or respiratory protection.

Here, then is how you prepare square stock: First, select your material. Serious woodworkers keep a stock on hand of materials they like to use. When I go to my wood merchant, I get to hand-select the planks that I want to buy, but I always try to buy approximately 100 board feet; this gives me price and delivery advantages (Illus. 4-1). Most of the time I work from the same materials anyway, so having excess material on hand is never really a problem. Furthermore, as prices keep escalating, having even a couple hundred board feet

Illus. 4-1. This good-looking stack of "shorts" consists of as much bird's-eye maple as I thought my car could carry. The longest pieces here are 58″ long.

of cherry on hand will save money in the long run.

I stack my selections in wood racks in my shop (Illus. 4-2), and then as I get ready to build a

project, I can select the material I want to work with (Illus. 4-3 and 4-4).

Next, cut the pieces to rough length (Illus. 4-5). I use a sabre rather than a circular saw for this operation, because I consider it quieter and less dangerous. Remember that the rough ends

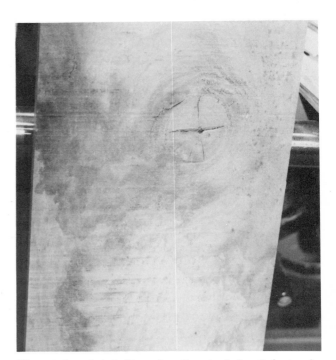

Illus. 4-2. Keeping your wood rack stocked with desirable timbers will save time and money.

Illus. 4-3 and 4-4. Examine the stock for defects. A knot like the one shown here is as unacceptable after planing (Illus. 4-4) as before.

Illus. 4-4.

Illus. 4-6. Be sure not to leave end-checking like this in your finished work; either cut narrow pieces around the crack or cut this whole end off the board.

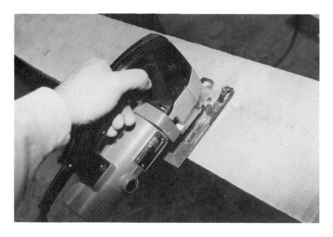

Illus. 4-5. I cut my stock with a sabre rather than a circular saw, because I believe it to be quieter and safer.

of boards are likely to be "checked" beyond use (Illus. 4-6). (A check is a lengthwise separation of the wood that usually extends across the rings of annual growth.) Also, note that the straightedge in Illus. 4-7 and 4-8 illustrates the twist and waves in the board; only by cutting it to appropriate

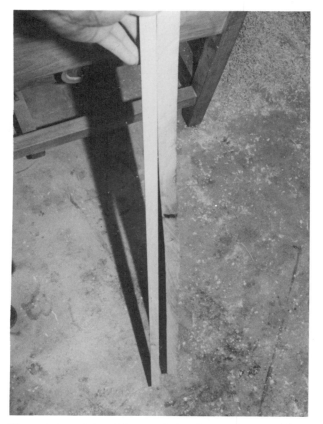

Illus. 4-7 and 4-8. The straightedge and saw table show twists and waves that might not be visible to the untrained eye. Boards like this must be cut to appropriate lengths if they are to provide much utility.

Illus. 4-8.

length before beginning to joint and plane it can
you get maximum use from this board.

Next, joint one edge clean (Illus. 4-9 and 4-10).
Then examine the ends of the piece; joint the
cupped side first (Illus. 4-11). If the stock is
cupped badly, it may be necessary to rip the piece
into a couple of narrower pieces, so the cupping
will be less pronounced. The first pass or two may
remove material only from the edges of the board

Illus. 4-10. Jointing one edge flat is the first step
towards seeing what is "inside" the stock.

Illus. 4-9. The first step in preparing any stock is
setting the fence on your jointer to absolutely
square.

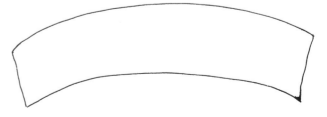

Illus. 4-11. Profile of a cupped board.

(Illus. 4-12–4-16). It's not necessary to joint *all* the way to a clean face; indeed, it's desirable to take at least the last pass off the jointed face with a planer (Illus. 4-17). This way, the board will be much smoother. Try to take an approximately equal amount off both faces of the board. The same amount doesn't necessarily mean the same number of passes, for your jointer passes are likely to be heavier than your planer passes.

Illus. 4-14.

Illus. 4-12. The next step is jointing one face.

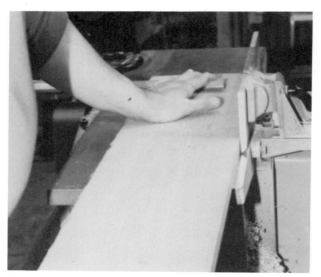

Illus. 4-13 and 4-14. Keep your hands as far as possible from the jointer's cutters.

Illus. 4-15 and 4-16. How a jointed face looks after a single pass.

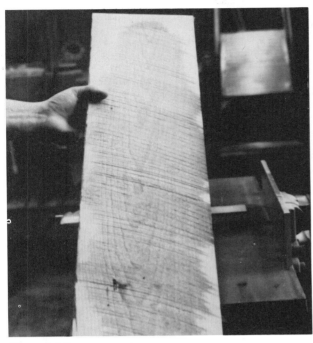

Illus. 4-16.

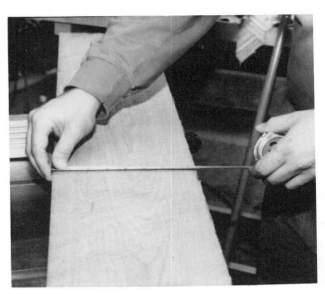

Illus. 4-18. Measure the stock's width for cutting.

Illus. 4-17. After jointing, the board does not have to be perfectly clean. If at all possible, the final cleanup should be in the planer.

Illus. 4-19. Then cut the stock to width.

Measure and saw the board to just over your desired width (Illus. 4-18 and 4-19), which may be ⅛″ narrower than the narrowest part of the board. There's no point in surfacing material you won't be using. Then check the material's thick-ness in the center of the board as well as on the edges. The piece in Illus. 4-20 is nearly 1⅜″ at the ruler, but only about 1 1/16″ at the edge of the board.

Wax your planer surface before you begin, to prevent losing a setting later on as you open the

Illus. 4-20. Check the thickness of the stock.

planer to wax it then. Then run all the pieces at the thickest setting (Illus. 4-21 and 4-22); you don't lose much time doing this, and you prevent any surprises or damage to the planer. The first pass may illustrate how variable are the thick and thin spots. Illus. 4-23–4-25 show the same panel after each of three passes. By the fourth pass (Illus. 4-26), the $1/16''$ passes can no longer be made in this very hard pecan material, so I started planing only half as much per pass. Illus. 4-27 shows a clean $15/16''$ surface. Now, advance to the other face.

After jointing one face so it is smooth, I plane the other face so it is smooth. Then I turn the

Illus. 4-21. Feed the stock into the planer.

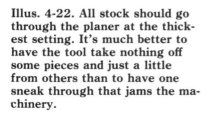

Illus. 4-22. All stock should go through the planer at the thickest setting. It's much better to have the tool take nothing off some pieces and just a little from others than to have one sneak through that jams the machinery.

Illus. 4-23–4-27. The stages in planing a board, from the uneven initial surface to the final clean pass.

Illus. 4-24.

Illus. 4-25.

Illus. 4-26.

Illus. 4-27.

board over with each pass through the planer (so that I take off *alternate* or opposite sides of the board) until the board reaches its desired thickness, which in this example is slightly more than ¾″, enough that I can sand to my heart's content and still have ¾″.

Joint one edge square to the new perfectly parallel faces (Illus. 4-28). You may have to start this jointing process at mid-board somewhere to get a very slightly concave rather than a very slight convex straight edge. This process can take several passes.

The material is now ready to be crosscut and ripped (Illus. 4-29). The capacity of my old INCA planer is about 6¼″, so I rip all pieces which will

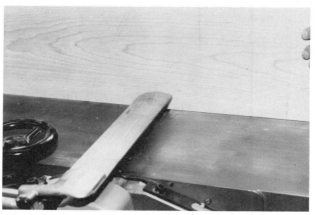

Illus. 4-28. After you have planed the stock to its desired thickness, rejoint one edge so that it is square to the now parallel surfaces.

Illus. 4-29. The stock is now ready for crosscutting, ripping, gluing, etc.

be glued into panels to about 6″; this way, I can plane the second edge absolutely parallel to the first. For panel-joining, I might take a couple of passes with a hand plane to permit "sprung" joints. A sprung joint has a gap of approximately one fine shaving that runs all but the first and last few inches of a joint. This gap is "sprung" under clamping pressure, and as the ends of the board dry out and shrink over time, panels so made have much less tendency to come apart at the glue joints. Some woodworkers cut out too much material when they "spring" a joint, and end up with a panel that is ⅛″ (or even more) narrower at the middle than at the end; certainly you don't want to do that!

Crosscut and glue the planed edges together. I use a couple of biscuits on the boards which force alignment, but in a longer panel, I'd use clamps like the Plano glue press as well to help ensure the flattest possible panel. This will minimize any work you may have to do later to flatten the panel.

Some woodworking authors have advised that you wipe up excess glue with a damp rag. Don't! This invariably leaves a mess that's invisible until it is time to finish the project. Others advise to let it harden completely. Cleaning up that glue is too much work! The best policy is to clean up the glue when it is about the texture of stiff cottage cheese. To do this, I use a chisel with its bevelled edge down, to prevent digging into the wood. What little of the glue that doesn't come up now very easily can be easily cleaned up later with a cabinet scraper.

5.
Gluing and Clamping Tabletops

Since most of us don't have access to wide planers or tools that work large material very easily, getting the stock flat in the preparation stage is essential. The previous chapter described how to flatten stock. The accompanying photos show a couple of ⅛″ dips in the stock, but they can be corrected in the gluing and clamping stages.

Start the operation by laying out all the pieces that are being considered for the top (Illus. 5-1). Arrange them to your liking, and then draw a large triangle that covers all the pieces (Illus. 5-2); this will help you to reassemble the tabletop (or other panel) properly.

Next, start jointing the edges that meet. In the example illustrated here, there are six pieces, so I will joint matching pairs of stock and have three separate gluings (Illus. 5-3–5-13). Enough jointing will be done so there's little point in turning off the jointer between pairs of boards. Be sure to leave slightly extra width so you have some to cut off; you'll lose width while jointing, and you'll have to cut material off the ends to square them up anyway. As you'll see, a flush trim router bit, drawn along a straightedge, leaves a nearly perfect edge after the top has been glued.

While it is possible to just glue the butt-jointed edges in place, most stock isn't really well enough prepared for that to be a viable option. Some stock can't be flattened perfectly, no matter how expertly you prepare it. So, let's consider some other methods of gluing and clamping the pieces so they are adequately flat. The easiest way is to never

Illus. 5-1. Lay out the boards in a pleasing pattern. Make sure that they line up.

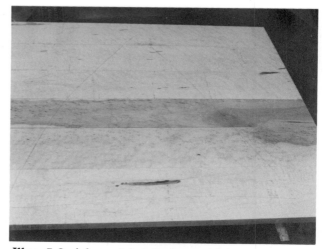

Illus. 5-2. A large triangle drawn with a pencil should mark your final, choice.

Illus. 5-3. Separate the planks into pairs for gluing.

Illus. 5-4. After appropriate jointing, glue each pair; note the clamp blocks which protect the edges which will be glued in the next operations.

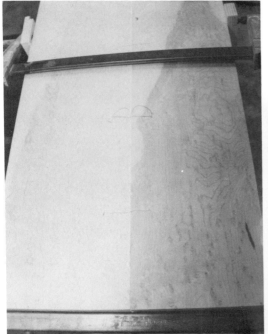

Illus. 5-5 (above left) . Then join two of the already-glued units. Illus. 5-6 (above right). Finally, glue the third "pair" onto the total piece.

Illus. 5-7. I set the whole panel in the shop's door-way, so the sun would expedite the glue drying—and, of course, to have the panel out of the way while I did some other operations.

Illus. 5-8. Scrape away excess glue with a painter's scraper.

Illus. 5-9. After using the scraper, clean up with a chisel.

Illus. 5-10 (above left). If the piece you've glued is fairly clean, you may cut off its excess length and trim the piece to size with a flush trimming bit and a router. Illus. 5-11 (above right). If you've glued successfully, the narrow piece you cut off will break in the wood rather than in the glue joints when you strike it against the bench.

Illus. 5-12. If you can remember to clamp your straight edge on with the clamp bars up, they won't be in your face as you do the routing.

Illus. 5-13. With the right straight edge (here the factory edge of a sheet of plywood) and a sharp flush trim bit, you can get a very nicely jointed edge without having to hoist the now heavy panel onto the jointer.

glue more than two pieces together at a time (unless you are using a clamping aid like the Plano glue press).

Another method is to use joining biscuits, which make great alignment aids even if you aren't gluing them. Since the top has to be very strong, glue these in place (Illus. 5-14–5-21). Five biscuits, the outer ones placed fairly near the ends, draw the pairs quite flat. Glue up the pairs of pieces. Make sure you have adequate clamping. This first round of clamping is usually pretty easy; most shops have plenty of clamps 12″ or smaller; gluing a piece four or five feet wide (or long) is much more a problem. Note the pads on the clamps in the illustrations; using the pads makes the next round of clamping much easier.

Clear away the small amount of glue squeeze-out while it is still the texture of cottage cheese; this is the easiest and most efficient time to do this. Then joint the remaining edges, and add biscuits to and glue two of the remaining three pieces together. After the glue has set, joint, add biscuits to, and glue the third pair of pieces to complete the top.

If you have access to a clamp like the Plano glue press (available from Advanced Machinery Imports, Ltd., P.O. Box 312, New Castle, Delaware), you may be successful at gluing more than two pieces together at a time. The Plano glue press is made for gluing up panels that are up to either 43″ or 49″ wide by any length. The width of each extruded aluminum clamp bar is 1⅜″. The maximum thickness that can be clamped is 4⅝″; perhaps even more interesting, the minimum that can be clamped is about 1/16″, which I can't imagine clamping **any** other way. While the Plano glue press is the premier edge clamp, it's also an effective veneering clamp when used with flat, stiff sheet stock for backing.

Because pressure is applied to all four sides of the joint at once, the Plano glue press flattens joints, even if some of the stock is slightly warped. These joints will still not be perfectly flat—slight cleanup may still be required, though not nearly as much as needed when gluing with pipe clamps,

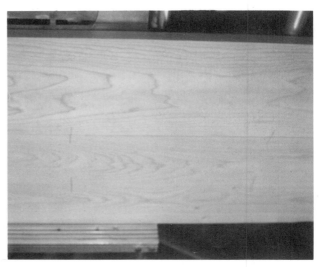

Illus. 5-14. The process is quite similar with heavy stock, which I now hesitate to glue without the Plano glue press. The scribed lines in this 2″ stock (which became the top of my new workbench) represent biscuit alignments.

Illus. 5-15. Glue each piece.

Illus. 5-16. When the piece is in the clamp, add the biscuits.

Illus. 5-17. As the clamp head is set in place, the glue begins to squeeze out.

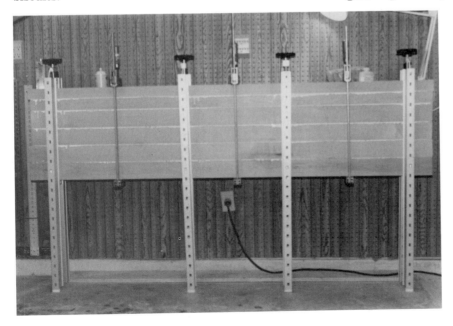

Illus. 5-18. Here the entire work-bench top is glued up; note the "standard" clamps between the members of the Plano glue press.

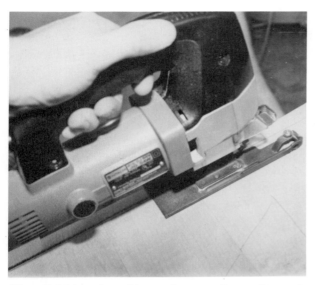

Illus. 5-19. Again, with a sabre saw I cut off nearly all the excess length.

Illus. 5-21. As usual, this is an instance where I'd be better off if I could remember to glue these trim-guide pieces on "upside-down," for that would make them "right-side up" when I do the cutting.

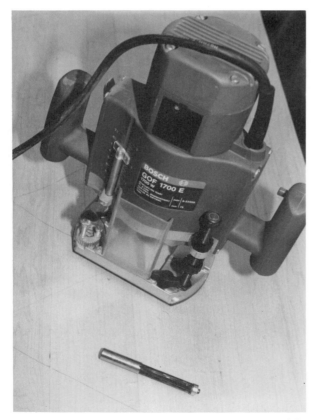

Illus. 5-20. Then I set up a heavy-duty router with a 2″ flush trim bit, to cut the ends square and true.

bar clamps, dowels, splines, or even biscuits. Also, panel construction of any kind is far quicker with the Plano glue press than with any of these other methods. For instance, I was able to quickly clean up a 32″ x 36″ panel I made with just a random orbital sander. Since the clamp provides uniform pressure over the entire width of the glue joint, bonding should be superior, especially if you've been one of those woodworkers who sometimes doesn't remember to alternate clamps from side to side of a panel as you glue it.

To use the Plano glue press, rest the clamp heads on the rear bar and set the clamp dogs so they are in the appropriate holes. Drop the glued pieces to be clamped in the top, resting them against the wall-mounted edge. You can very safely use slightly less glue than you otherwise might have used. Working quickly is essential, because the press will force the panels flat, even if the glue has begun to set. The Plano glue press is ideal for gluing "sprung" joints, those that have been planed slightly concave so that as the material dries out with age, the joints' ends don't open.

If your jointer is set up properly, it will make a truly flat surface that should be ready for gluing without the need to "spring" the joints. The bird's-eye maple top photographed in this chapter was glued without my having to "spring" the joints with a hand plane.

Though biscuit-joined panels are better aligned and stronger than butt-joined panels, there are other ways to achieve the same result. One of these methods involves using a shaper and a glue-joint cutter like Freud's #EC-031 (Illus. 5-22). You'll have to make a couple of passes to ensure proper alignment, but once you do, you'll be gluing straight, flat panels which have nearly twice the gluing surface of the butt joints that I biscuit together; the edges made by the glue joint cutter provide at least as much aligning help as do the joining biscuits. I use the biscuit joiner in preference to this because I hesitate to dedicate my shaper simply for this task, and I'm usually in too much of a hurry to do the setup. Of course, it might be less expensive in a hobby shop to do the setup than to use dozens of biscuits.

There are router bits which also make a glue joint cut, among them the CMT #855-501 bit. As with the just-mentioned shaper setup, you'll have to make a couple of passes to get the desired results, but this may be the ideal setup for you, especially if you have a router for your router table that you can dedicate for this use. It's important that big bits like this be used *only* in the router table; you'll get much better work bringing the work to the bit rather than vice versa.

Finally, there is the Porter-Cable model 692 Tru-Match edge-joining system for solid-surface materials (Illus. 5-23), which also works quite well on wood. This system consists of a sub-base for a Porter-Cable or Rockwell router which has a step for precisely setting the Tru-Match bit-cutting depth without changing the bit adjustment in the router. After setting up this router base, one can rout the "high" side of the cut off one side of the router, and the "low" side off the other. One advantage of this system is that it can be run freehand against a fence rather than in a router table. The wavy cuts this bit makes are different enough from other cuts to provide an interesting change of pace.

Illus. 5-22. Note the difference in size between the glue-joint shaper bit (right) and the glue joint router bit.

Illus. 5-23. The Porter-Cable Tru-Match System; note the "wave" in the cutter and the split-level base; this is the only glue-joint system (other than biscuit joining) that can be operated freehand.

Planing, Sanding, and Finishing the Top

Glue removal should precede any machine or hand planing. As already noted, as much glue as possible should be removed with a scraper or chisel. After it has hardened, the glue is much harder than wood, and will cause premature wear or even chipping on your planing tools.

If the top is badly "out of flat," it's almost worth the cost of having it machined flat by someone who has a thickness planer wide enough to handle it. A 30″ thickness planer is the largest machine I know of in my area; for reasons other than price, I prefer to avoid using it whenever possible. Cutters this wide are difficult and expensive to maintain, and are, consequently, usually in fairly rough shape.

To flatten stock that is badly "out of flat," plane cross grain, checking the stock often with a straightedge and a square. If you really don't care to plane or if you don't have a suitable smoothing plane, you can do this operation nearly as well with a belt sander. The consequence is that you'll leave cross-grain scratches which will take extra long to remove once you belt-sand with the grain "properly" oriented.

Follow belt-sanding by sanding with a random orbital sander, if your shop has one, at the same grit you finished belt-sanding at. Keep the sander moving, because random orbital sanders are sufficiently aggressive to ruin a flat surface quickly.

After you have moved up a couple of grits with the random orbital sander, complete the sanding process with a regular palm sander or by hand. If I sand all the way to 320 or 440 grit, I prefer to do these sandings without the aid of a machine.

By the time the top is assembled completely, it's usually too large to pass over stationary tools. I'm not strong enough to accurately pass a 3′ x 4′ tabletop over my short-bed jointer, and there's no room for it even on my industrial-strength Uni-saw table saw. The ends and edges of these large pieces have to be cut and shaped with hand tools.

Since the tabletop has at least one jointed edge, I measure square from that edge, doing all marking on the panel's inferior side. Then I clamp a piece of *straight* scrap or other stock along the line I want cut. This is one time when it's a good idea to clamp with the clamp stems *up* rather than the usual way, so they will be *down* (rather than in your face) when you flip the piece for cutting. Be sure your flush trim bit is sharp, and use the shortest bit possible for the best results. As you master your proper work speed, you'll find that this sawing and routing will leave you with very good edges.

All that remains to be done with the tabletop now is to shape its edges (Illus. 5-24 and 5-25). I have curved both the tops and bottoms of the edges of many of my tables with a small-diameter round-over bit in a router. I wanted a different

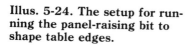

Illus. 5-24. The setup for running the panel-raising bit to shape table edges.

shape for the table illustrated, but a regular chamfer seemed too much, so I set up a raised panel bit, but used the router table's fence rather than the bit's bearing as a guide. I used only the flat portion of the bit, leaving no square edges on either the top or the bottom; the gentle degree of gentle chamfer provides a very satisfactory edge to the table.

Illus. 5-25. The tabletop with the partially "raised" panels.

6.
Joining Aprons to Legs

There are four principal ways of joining the aprons and legs on any table: mortise-and-tenon joints, steel corner joints, wood corner joints, and biscuit joints. Each offers some advantages and disadvantages. Whichever joint you choose has to be mechanically sound as well as able to hold glue; glue alone is never enough.

Mortise-and-tenon Joints
The first and perhaps foremost method of joining aprons and legs is the old standby, the mortise-and-tenon joint. This joint consists of a mortise and a tenon. The mortise is a slot into which the tenon is placed. Ideally, the tenon fits snug enough so that there's barely room for the glue, which

makes this joint mechanically sound. Many of the mortises used in apron/leg joinery are open all the way to the top (Illus. 6-1). Some mortises are haunched, which is to say they are cut to accept tenons that aren't just extensions of the stock; an example of this type of tenon is shown in Illus. 6-2. A good workbench like the one shown in Chap-

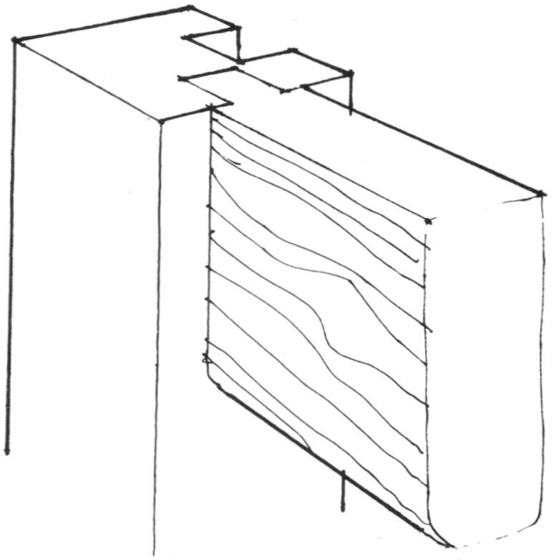

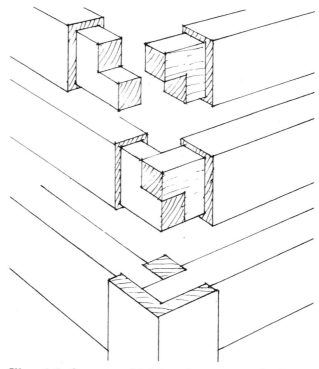

Illus. 6-1. Sometimes mortises for table aprons are open all the way to the top.

Illus. 6-2. One way of joining the apron to the legs. This type of mortise-and-tenon joint has a great deal of gluing surface, and is stronger mechanically than some other types of mortise-and-tenon joints.

ter 11 will prove helpful when you're sawing, chopping, and paring mortise-and-tenon joints. A bench dog clamping system is almost a necessity for performing these tasks.

Today, mortises are cut in a variety of ways. One could still chisel them out completely by hand using mortising chisels against a marked line. Even the very strong find that they tire quickly doing this physical work, which demands great precision. Mortise chisels are very thick and you can use them without damaging them. However, since the best of these have wooden handles, use wood or neoprene mallets; metal mallets would damage the tools' handles pretty quickly.

More in tune with today's woodworking practices, we could make the mortises with a drill press and a stop (Illus. 6-3), either by drilling repeated holes (preferably with brad-point bits, which wander less) and cleaning between them with chisels (Illus. 6-4), or by running a spiral router bit up and down a channel (Illus. 6-5 and 6-6), taking very little material with each new

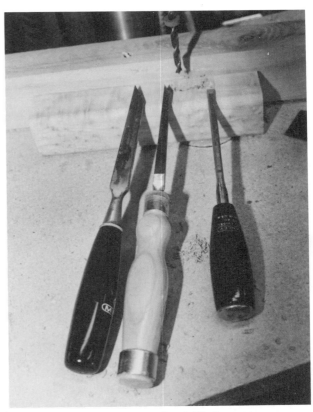

Illus. 6-4. The block with the drilled mortise supports three types of chisels. From left to right, they are the very thick full mortise chisel, the "registered" mortise chisel, and a standard chisel.

Illus. 6-3. Drilling a marked mortise with the drill press.

Illus. 6-5. Mortises can be cut faster and neater if you mount a spiral router bit rather than a drill bit in your drill press. Note the featherboard in the foreground; it helps to keep the work lined up square and straight, and prevents kickbacks.

Illus. 6-6. A pair of
mortises ready to
accept tenons with
mitred ends.

Illus. 6-8. A view of the squaring process.

pass. While this second way produces a very satisfactory slot, it is a slot that ends with round
corners; the alternatives are to square the corner
with a chisel (Illus. 6-7 and 6-8), or to file the
tenon round at the end (Illus. 6-9). This isn't important when ordinary mortises are involved, but
it becomes more critical when "through" mortises
are used (like those shown on the computer desk
in Chapter 14); square tenons are more "traditional," while "round" tenons are considered

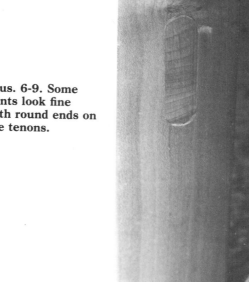

Illus. 6-9. Some
joints look fine
with round ends on
the tenons.

Illus. 6-7. Mount the piece to be mortised in a vise
before you begin to chop the corners square.

more "contemporary." If you have many tenons to cut, a router can be used in place of the drill press, and there are a variety of jigs and fixtures which help to make this process much simpler. It's useful to use featherboards to help keep the work both straight and true when drilling these joints in a drill press.

A particularly effective way to cut these mortises is to use a router that has been set up with *two* edge guides (Illus. 6-10–6-12). Set the width of cut with the adjusters on the guides, and then position the cut with the adjusters right on the router's base.

There are square chisel mortisers available for running on your drill press (Illus. 6-13 and 6-14), and a couple of manufacturers are currently re-marketing dedicated mortisers; if your wood-working requires lots of square corner tenons, an inexpensive unit will likely pay for itself in no time.

The tenons can be cut in the apron pieces either by hand or with a variety of jigs. They can be cut with a small backsaw, freehand with a band saw,

Illus. 6-10. A view of the end grain on the leg set on the router between two edge guides.

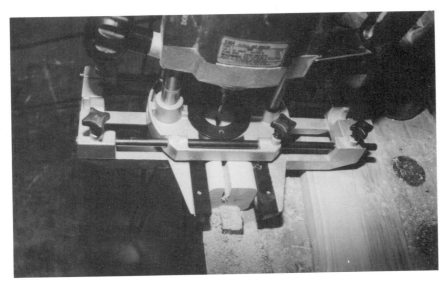

Illus. 6-11. A router is being used to cut this configuration.

Illus. 6-12. The results are the cleanest possible mortises.

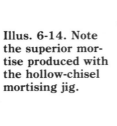

Illus. 6-14. Note the superior mortise produced with the hollow-chisel mortising jig.

Illus. 6-13. A chisel mortiser like this makes the mortise-and-tenon joint much more reasonable to make. When used with the twin-blade tenon jig in Illus. 6-15 and described in Chapter 7, it will produce as good a joint as possible.

or with a table saw and a tenon jig. Perhaps the best of the jigs is the two-blade model described in Chapter 7 and shown in Illus. 6-15. Cutting haunches on the tenons is simply a matter of making another pair of strokes with the saw to remove

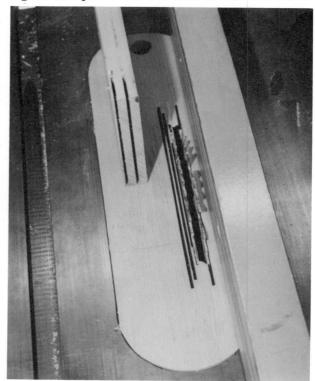

Illus. 6-15. Cutting a tenon with the two-blade jig.

a (small) corner of the wood. Some other tenons are made to meet inside mortises. Mitring these tenons helps to fill the mortises, and full mortises make a mechanically stronger joint, which in turn means you'll have to rely less on your glue. Illus. 6-16 shows a mitred mortise-and-tenon joint from which a single-blade width of too much material was removed; after the table is assembled, no one will see this error, but it will certainly compromise the long-term strength of the project. Whenever you're cutting tenons, it's certain that having to pare away some material is superior to having to shim the tenon in place in the mortise; the shim would greatly reduce the joint's strength.

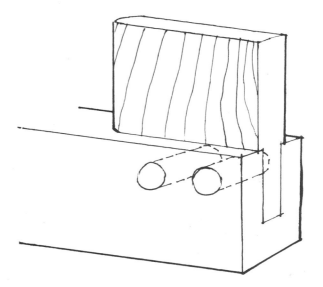

Illus. 6-17. Another way to make your joints strong is to "pin" the tenon.

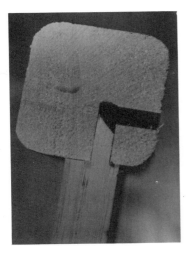

Illus. 6-16. The tenon on this mortise-and-tenon joint has been mitred one blade thickness too short. Over time, the joint's strength will be compromised.

Another way of making sure your joints are mechanically strong is to "pin" the tenons, as shown in Illus. 6-17. When this is done with contrasting woods, it can be extremely attractive, particularly if the style of furniture complements it. On the other hand, while the pin must be tight in the leg, the hole it passes through in the tenon must be loose enough to allow for the wood's seasonal movement; if you don't make this allowance, the project will, sooner or later, break at the pinning point.

Corner Braces

There are several reasons to use steel corner braces (Illus. 6-18) rather than mortise-and-tenon joints, biscuit joints, or wood block corners. If you

Illus. 6-18. An end view of the corner brace and a hanger bolt joint.

hope to make the table transportable, removable legs are essential; hanger bolts and wing nuts are an obvious and *very* satisfactory answer to the problem.

Woodcraft's corner braces are more substantial than others I have seen because they require six screws be driven into the aprons at each corner, rather than the more usual one. To install these braces a 3/32″ wide x 1/4″ deep saw kerf must be cut parallel to each leg. I cut these kerfs about 2½″ from the ends, though you might want to vary that distance based on the thickness of your table's legs. If these slots are to be cut in apron pieces of different lengths or if you don't have a length-setting stop on your crosscut gauge, you might use a shim to set the distance accurately for these repeated cuts.

After the slots were cut, I drilled pilot holes for screws in the slots and installed corner brackets in the slots with screws (Illus. 6-19). If you are making more than one table base at a time, you may want to use a self-centering drill bit like the one shown in Illus. 6-20.

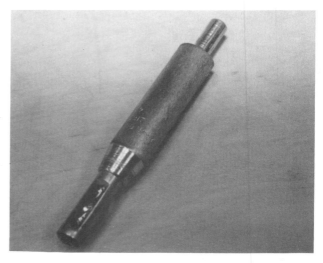

Illus. 6-20. Using a self-aligning bit like the Vix-Bit® helps to ensure accurate hole placement which, in turn, leads to steadier table bases.

Illus. 6-19. Install the corner brackets in the slots with screws; the "Yankee" screwdriver is being used here. This screwdriver is a precursor to the battery-operated "cordless" screwdrivers of today.

Drilling the legs for the hanger bolts can be done freehand, or it can be more squarely done in a V-block on the drill press, as shown in Illus. 6-21 and 6-22. Drill the holes 1½″ from the top on the inside corner of the leg. Clamp the V-block to the drill-press table so the correct drilling spot is directly under the drill bit. Use a scrap block at the end of the V-block to position the end of the piece to be drilled accurately. Hanger bolts that are 5/16″ are *far* stronger than 1/4″ hanger bolts for mounting legs to aprons through these factory-made corners.

After the legs have been drilled for the hanger bolts, attach the hanger bolts with a nut driver by simply applying a cap nut to the bolt end of the nut (Illus. 6-23–6-25); if you can find steel cap nuts, they'll be less likely to break under repeated use than are the more readily available (and more expensive) brass cap nuts.

Attach all four legs to the apron with wing nuts (Illus. 6-26). Though I had done everything in my power to ensure a square setup, I wasn't completely satisfied with the table base's flatness before I fastened the top. It seems to me that when making this table, I used the top to ensure the flatness of the rest of the work.

Illus. 6-21 (above left). Use a jig like this to drill hanger bolts when you use the corner block method of assembling a table's base. Illus. 6-22 (above right). This view shows the chips beng swept from the jig as a new piece is being installed; this is why the end cap which determines the depth is not attached.

Illus. 6-23. Put the hanger bolts into the legs with cap nuts or a pair of jammed nuts; here a pair of nuts is being jammed together by being turned tight in opposite directions.

Illus. 6-24 and 6-25. While one could simply turn the hanger bolt into the drilled hole, the process goes faster and easier if you turn the leg rather than just the wrench.

Illus. 6-25.

Illus. 6-26. This close-up of the leg/apron/top assembly shows that the legs are attached with corner irons and wing nuts, and the table fasteners positioned near the corners.

Using Biscuit Joints

Another method worth considering is biscuiting the apron to the legs. Chopping a couple of sets of mortises by hand reminded me how much I really prefer biscuit joinery for many of these joints. Biscuit joints are also stronger. I recently made one too many leg sets using the biscuit method, and I decided to take one of the leg sets apart. I beat at it with a rubber hammer for several minutes before I gave up and cut the piece apart with a table saw, setting the saw about 1/32″ larger than the legs.

First, mark out the joints (Illus. 6-27). Doing this is always important, but it's crucial if your apron is narrow. Then, if you want a ¼″ inset where the apron meets the legs, use a ¼″ spacer pad big enough to balance your joiner when cutting there.

Illus. 6-27. Lay out the biscuit cut with a small pencil line like this.

Next, set the joiner to make the first cut on the legs. Don't use the spacer yet. Make *all* the leg cuts (Illus. 6-28). Then, with the spacer in place, make the apron cuts; again, continue all the way around the table (Illus. 6-29).

Next, set up for a second cut; this one should be at least ¼″ from the outside (visible) edge. Setting the cuts ¼″ apart on the tool's scale provides this spacing. Make the cuts. When glued and biscuited, this joint will be as strong as any joint discussed in this chapter. As Illus. 6-30 indicates, ¼″ offset won't be enough if you do much rounding over of the corners; be sure to plan for this before you cut.

Illus. 6-28. To cut the off-set biscuit joint between the leg and apron, cut the leg using only the joiner's guide.

Illus. 6-29. Then cut the apron piece with a shim in place; the piece of ¼″ plywood used here is almost so large as to obscure the apron piece in the photograph.

Illus. 6-30. The finished joint will be as strong as any other you could make.

7.
Tenoning and Taper Jigs

Tenoning Jig

The mortise-and-tenon joint is still considered by many woodworkers to be the best way to join table aprons to legs. When these joints had to be cut by hand, making them was a time-consuming practice. With the advent of power tools, many jigs have been devised to help make these joints more easily. Most table-saw manufacturers offer fancy accessory jigs for tenoning. These position the work for cutting one cheek of the tenon at a time. Here's a method that's superior to using those jigs, for it provides tenons that are uniform in thickness and easily repeatable.

Make spacer discs for the size of tenon you will most commonly use. With a great deal of help, I used a friend's metal-cutting lathe to make spacer

discs for $\frac{1}{4}''$, $\frac{5}{16}''$, $\frac{3}{8}''$, and $\frac{1}{2}''$ tenons. I used $2\frac{3}{4}''$-diameter round steel stock, drilling a $\frac{5}{8}''$ arbor hole exactly in the middle to preserve balance; absolutely no wobble is acceptable in this setup. When you make your spacer discs, you may have to vary the size by a few hundredths of an inch to allow for the set of the blades you use; mine are all a few hundredths of an inch oversize to allow for the hollow-ground planer blades that I use. By measuring a set tooth and a spot near the arbor hole with a dial indicator, you can determine precisely how oversize your spacer discs must be. Alternatively, bring the blades with you if you have the discs made, so the machinist can do this measuring.

Illus. 7-1. The materials needed for double-blade tenoning consist of a pair of blades, a spacer disc, and a table saw.

Before their very first use, the blades should be sharpened and only very slightly set at the same time, *as though they were a single blade rather than individual ones;* they *must* be *exactly* alike.

First, insert the blades in the saw. Illus. 7-1 shows that in addition to the spacer, I use the flange that accompanies the arbor nut. After tightening the blades, insert a shop-made throat plate in the saw; I make several of these at a time, of pine or other softwood, and cut them to a precise thickness so they are uniform with the top of the saw. When using a new throat plate, turn on the saw with the blades below the table; then elevate the spinning blades slowly so they may cut through the throat plate. You may find that you like these close-fitting throat plates so well that you'll want to use them all the time.

Set your depth of cut carefully using measured spacer blocks or a tool setup gauge. Then set the saw's fence or a taller auxiliary fence accurately and squarely. Now you're ready to cut your pieces.

The pair of saw blades will cut uniform tenons on all the pieces for whatever job you have.

Illus. 7-2 and 7-3 show tenons being cut over the two blades. If there are to be tenons on both ends of your pieces, flip them end over end so the same edge meets the fence; this ensures that you get a flat surface if many tenons are being used in a row. After removing one of the blades, carefully set up your mitre gauge and the blade at the correct height and cut away the scrap cheeks (Illus. 7-4 and 7-5).

This method of cutting tenons is much quicker than other methods. On the day I took the photos illustrated in this chapter, I cut matching tenons on both ends of 39 pieces in just under 20 minutes—including setup time! Not only was this a terrific timesaver, but it also gave me 78 joints that fit perfectly the first time.

Taper Jig

In this section, I describe how to make two varieties of taper jig. Taper jigs are used to cut tapers,

Illus. 7-2 (above left). The vertical cut on a small tenon. A raised fence would make this operation more accurate. Illus. 7-3 (above right). Side view of the vertical cut on the small tenon.

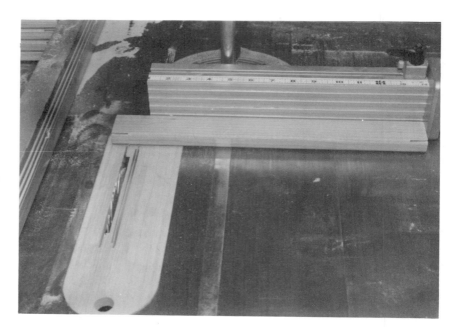

Illus. 7-4. The setup for the horizontal cuts is much easier if you have a mitre gauge with an accurate stop system.

Illus. 7-5. After many tenons have been cut, lots of cheek parts can accumulate on your saw's table.

inclined surfaces along the edge of a board. The first jig is very simple to make (Illus. 7-6–7-10). Square up two 1 x 2s; nominal dimensions are being used, so anything much wider than 1½″ will be terrific. Put the two pieces in the vise. Fasten the hinge to one end. Cut a slight angle in what will become the front of the work-support piece; this gives it just a bit of "bite" when you're using the jig. Glue or dowel the work-support piece to one side of the hinged pair (or fasten it with *brass* fasteners); it's important to use soft fasteners and to make the work-support piece easily replaceable, for there will be cuts where the saw enters this piece.

Cutting List for the Taper Jig

Part	Quantity	Thickness	Width	Length
Main Body	2	³/₄″	2″	20″
Work-Support Piece with Slight Taper	1	³/₄″	1½″	2″
Angle-Set Adjusting Piece	1	½″	1″	6″
Hinge	1		1½″	1½″
Hanger Bolt with Fender Washer and Wing Nut; Screws	1			

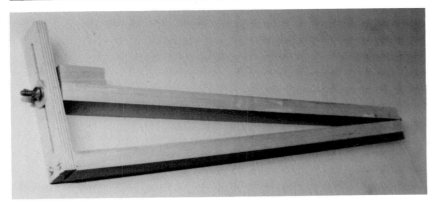

Illus. 7-6. A simple taper jig.

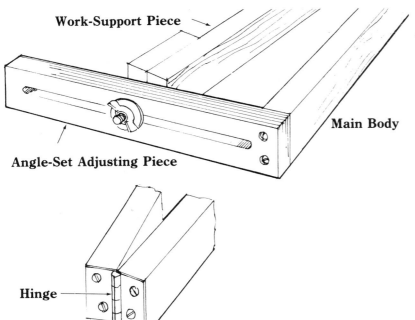

Work-Support Piece

Main Body

Angle-Set Adjusting Piece

Hinge

Illus. 7-7. Drawings of the simple taper jig.

Illus. 7-8. The simple taper jig in action.

Illus. 7-9 and 7-10. Close-up of both ends of the simple taper jig.

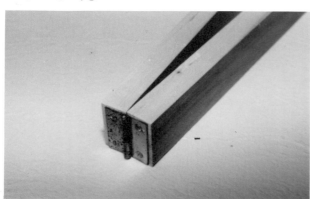

Illus. 7-10.

Rout a 4 to 5″ long, ¼″ slot down the middle of the 1″ x 6″ plywood piece that will be used for setting angles; I found this quite easy to do on the drill press with a spiral router bit.

In the 20″-long work-support piece, drill a 3/16″-hole. Jam two nuts on a hanger bolt by hand-screwing them both onto the thread, and then tightening them into one another. Use these jammed nuts to steady the wrench as you drive the lag screw end of the hanger bolt into the hole. Then release and remove the nuts.

Set the angle-setting piece on the ends of the jig, over the hanger bolt; add a fender washer and a wing nut; then screw the piece to the piece that rides the fence. Some woodworkers may want to cut some pieces to slip inside the jig to ensure that it doesn't close slightly in use; others will use these blocks to ensure accurate repetitive cuts.

Now, you're ready to cut some tapers. However, you should be aware of one thing: Your fingers get perilously close to the saw blade as you guide the work through the saw, so use this jig with push sticks and only if you are going to cut a few tapers. If you're building many tables, you'll much prefer to make the following changes to the taper jig: Make the piece that rides the fence at least 3½″ wide. Mount the angle-setting piece to the top, using hanger bolts and wing nuts on both sides for an easy setup. Add a clamp like the one shown in Illus. 7-11; it is much better to spend a few dollars for a clamp like this than to have your hands so close to the saw blade. These clamps are readily available from all the major woodworking supply houses. Finally, add a handle that will ensure that you're pushing from a spot where there's no chance of contacting the blade. Illus. 7-12 shows the jig in use.

Illus. 7-11. The more-elaborate taper jig may interfere with the guard on your table saw, depending on the width of the stock to be cut. Frankly, I prefer this jig, even if used with a guard, to the simpler version.

Illus. 7-12. Tapers that you have drawn on the wood can be set at one of the saw table's mitre gauge slots.

8.
Cutting Dovetails by Hand

Hand-cut through dovetails provide a strong, handsome joint for carcass work, and they do appear in at least one of our tables. Variable spacing makes the joint as decorative as it is strong. The dovetail joint is sometimes recognized as the "hallmark" of quality furniture, but this isn't necessarily the case. Sloppily made dovetails are every bit as unattractive as sloppily made joinery of any other kind. Most woodworkers' first experiences with dovetails are so frustrating, they either quit making dovetails altogether or manage to make some inferior ones on rare occasions. But the dovetail doesn't have to be the exclusive province of "artistic" woodworkers. By following these steps, you will become proficient at cutting dovetails by hand. Additionally, as you learn to make these joints you will adapt a care and precision that will appear in other aspects of your work. And while you won't cut dovetails rapidly when you first start, using the method described here, you will eventually be able to cut both the pins and tails of varibly spaced dovetails at the general rate of about two feet per hour.

Tools Needed

Through dovetails cannot be made without the right tools. You will need a marking gauge for scribing precisely located lines parallel to the ends of the boards. You also need an angle-marking gauge. There are a few possibilities here. You can use the traditional wing-nut marking gauge and set it so the angle bar crosses a square held against the other side eight inches from the beginning; this is an angle of 8°. If, like me, you have other uses for this tool as you continue working on a table project, you may want an angle-marking gauge that can be used as both a straightedge and at a setting of 8°. The Veritas marking gauge is an inexpensive adjunct to your square; some woodworkers might regard the more expensive Bridge City gauge superior because it provides both an angle and a square.

You will also need a saw to cut the dovetails. My Sears dovetail saw is my favorite dovetailing saw. When it comes back from sharpening, I lay its blade between a pair of boards and hammer out most of the set; saws that cut narrow kerfs do a better job of dovetailing. I've used Japanese saws with mixed satisfaction. I've also used a brass-backed back saw and have been unhappy with the results. If you can operate your band saw *very* efficiently, and if that band saw is capable of cutting precisely square, you may want to use it. Often, I set my band saw to 8° off square in each direction and cut the pins for a project, but I only do this if the boards are of manageable length and are narrow enough to fit within the band-saw's throat.

Dovetailing also requires bevel-backed chisels. Extensive dovetailing will require a set of chisels that range from $1/8''$ to $1\frac{1}{2}''$ wide by eighths of an inch. They should, of course, be razor-sharp (Illus. 8-1). My old Stanley 040C chisels withstand the abuses of dovetailing better than any other chisels I have used.

Use a carver's mallet rather than a hammer to strike the chisel. You'll find the work far less fatiguing because the mallet seems to deliver more even blows to the chisel. My favorite is a 27-ounce bronze mallet because it has a big handle and a

Illus. 8-1. Before you begin to cut dovetail joints, make sure your chisels are sharp.

small head that give me excellent control when removing waste.

You will also need a straightedge and a pair of clamps to hold it and the work down on your bench. The straightedge should be a piece of 2 x 2 as long as the width of any piece you might ever dovetail; it should be perfectly square and perfectly flat, and one face of it should have some "medium" (#100 or 120-grit) sandpaper glued onto it. This straightedge is clamped facedown on the sawed board when the waste is removed with the chisels.

A marking knife is also needed. A layout could not be done as well with a pencil. Finally, while it's not essential to use a particular kind of glue, I find that hide glue used in a glue pot is easy to use, easy to clean up after, and does the best job of filling any imperfections in my cutting.

Dovetail-cutting Techniques

The most important part of this job is marking out the joint. Start by using your marking gauge to measure the thickness of the piece which is to have the "tails" cut on it. Then scribe a line on all four faces of the board that is to have the "pins" cut on it; this line should extend across the end

of the board (Illus. 8-2). Deciding just where to put the marks is probably the most "creative" part of the job. I usually do the layout with a ruler before starting the actual marking. This helps to ensure that my spacings are even on both ends of the board, that they are symmetrical on each end, and that the waste can be chopped with my chisels. Typically, I measure from both edges of the board, and, even if most of the "pins" are of uniform size, the middle several pins may be wider or narrower than the others.

Illus. 8-2. Use a marking gauge to scribe a line across the end of the board to be dovetailed. The line should be positioned so it marks the thickness of the other piece in the dovetail.

Next, take your dovetail gauge and mark out the pin spacings on the end of the board (Illus. 8-3). After the ends are marked, use a small square to extend the marks down both faces of the board. I find it helpful to mark the waste areas with X's. There are two methods of marking out the other piece. In the first, everything is marked at once and cut perfectly. In the second, the pins are cut completely and then the tails are marked from them. The second method is more realistic because sawing is often imperfect.

Illus. 8-3. Use a dovetail gauge like this one from Bridge City Tools to mark the pins. First you mark the end at opposing angles, and then you connect those marks to the scribed line. The Bridge City gauge is ideal because it offers both the correct angle and a straight edge.

Saw on the waste side of the lines just down to the scribed line with whichever type of saw you use (Illus. 8-4). Stay on the waste side of the line.

Before you proceed with the dovetailing, stop to make sure your chisels have been honed. The next step will be much more effective with sharp

Illus. 8-4. With a backsaw, cut on the waste side of each line.

tools—and you will be much less likely to hurt yourself or damage your project with sharp chisels. Before you begin chiselling out the waste, clamp the board onto the end of your bench with the straightedge clamped exactly on the scribed line (Illus. 8-5). Chisel out the waste stock, using the clamped-on straightedge as a square. Having a variety of chisels makes this operation easier.

Illus. 8-5. Position the cut piece under a straight-edge, with the straightedge riding your scribed line exactly. I used a piece of 2″-thick stock to help ensure that my chisel stays straight during the dovetailing operation.

You need to establish a rhythm for this chopping. I count as if I'm counting the beats to music and land a mallet blow with each "beat." Usually, I work all the way across the board vertically, from left to right, six to eight strokes per waste area (Illus. 8-6). Then I work back from right to left, removing waste stock from each area by tapping the chisel into the waste horizontally (Illus. 8-7). I then follow this with another round of vertical chops and then remove the chips with horizontal chops. I continue this until I am just over halfway through the board; at this point, one more row of vertical blows signals the need to turn the board over (Illus. 8-8). I repeat this procedure on the other side of the board (Illus. 8-9). The straight-

Illus. 8-6. The first chisel strokes are vertical.

Illus. 8-7. The next chisel strokes are horizontal.

Illus. 8-8. After you have removed about half the material, turn the piece over.

Illus. 8-9. Cut again vertically with the chisel until each piece of waste stock is removed.

edge helps to ensure that the work is square or perhaps slightly concave on the chiselled edge; a convex surface wouldn't work at all here, because it would cause gaps.

Mark out the mating piece as soon as all the "pins" have been cut. Stand the pieces at right angles to one another, and scribe the exact size and shape of the pins onto the board where you will soon cut the tails (Illus. 8-10). Again, I mark X's on the waste areas. With these pieces, it is especially important to cut on the waste side of the line (Illus. 8-11).

After you have cut your newly scribed lines,

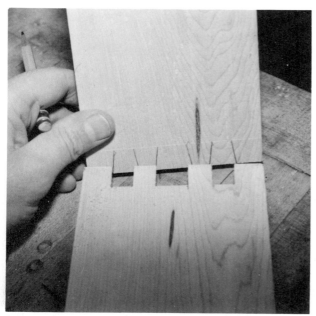

Illus. 8-10. Line up the other board with the piece you have just cut. With a knife, mark the piece with a pencil, as shown here. Quickly put some identifying marks in the areas you will cut away.

Illus. 8-11. With a handsaw or a band saw, carefully cut away the waste pieces, always on the waste side of the line.

again remove the waste stock exactly on the "pin" pieces, with first vertical, and then horizontal chisel cuts, or by using a band saw (Illus. 8-12).

Illus. 8-12. You can either chisel out the waste after cutting or you can remove it one saw kerf at a time with the band saw, as shown here.

If you have marked out carefully, your dovetails should go together with little or no fitting (Illus. 8-13 and 8-14). Sometimes you may find that one or more of the tails may be either too big or too small for the pin. If you cannot have a perfect fit, it is better to have a tail that is too big; this way, all you have to do is pare it. Use a freshly honed chisel to remove the excess wood that keeps the joint from fitting; ensure that the pins and tails fit loose enough that you needn't hammer the joint together, and fit tight enough that the joint will hold together without adhesive.

If there is a gap between the pins and tails, your next step will depend upon the size of the gap. If the gap is narrower than the thickness of the kerf of your dovetail saw, go ahead and glue the pieces together; you will solve the "gap" problems as the glue is setting.

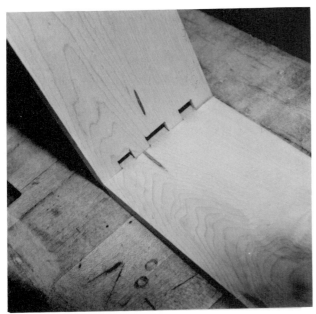

Illus. 8-13. After the cutting has been completed, test-fit the pieces together.

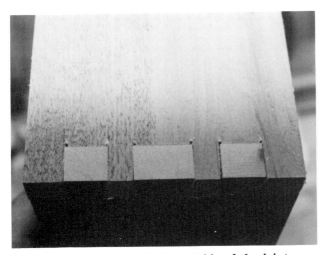

Illus. 8-14. This view of the outside of the joint shows that it is ready to be glued.

ature, you will no longer need to clamp the joint to ensure that it stays put. This is the main reason for my preference for "pot" glue for dovetailing.

Patching is a topic that is rarely discussed, but most woodworkers make mistakes, and should learn how to hide them so that they are not noticeable (Illus. 8-15). While your glue is setting, try to pull a small piece of veneer through any gaps; if it is too tight, make a saw kerf right through the glue. Though this sounds like it might make a mess, it works! Just make sure you have a good coat of wax on the saw and that you wash the glue off the blade immediately after this operation. Then put some glue on both sides of the piece of veneer. It just happens that most veneer is the same thickness as the kerf of the average dovetail saw. There is a school of thought that suggests that all the dovetails should be patched in this way with a contrasting wood, to add a decorative effect.

If there are void spots in the joint, you may want to inject some glue into them. Also, it is a good idea to start cleaning up while the glue is still about the texture of cottage cheese. The neater the job at this stage, the easier the rest of the project will be. Cleaning up this joint can be as easy or as difficult as the individual woodworker wants to make it. Certainly chisels, cabinet scrap-

Illus. 8-15. This other view shows that there is a need for one small patch (on the bottom left area of the joint) to make this joint quite presentable and very strong. A perfectionist would, of course, suggest that it's time to recut the piece.

Gluing is a fairly straightforward part of the operation. Using "pot" glue will help you learn to work quickly. Cover all mating surfaces with glue. Press the pieces together, hold them briefly, and by the time the glue has cooled to room temperers, and a plane are permissible to use. Often, I use a belt sander because it's quick and neat. As a last step in this clean-up process, I like to put a small chamfer along the corner of each dovetail. Two fine plane shavings followed by a few strokes with a piece of fine sandpaper chamfers these corners just enough.

Cutting your first set of dovetails will seem to take forever and you will be frustrated with the results, which will seem less than perfect. Don't despair: I had cut only about two feet of dovetails in my entire career when I took a commission to build a suite of furniture that had approximately 72 running feet of dovetails. It was building that project that made me proficient at cutting what has become my favorite joint. Practise my method and you will soon be able to cut fine dovetails at a surprising pace.

9.
Gluing, Sanding, and Finishing

Do as much sanding, planing, or scraping on the project as you can before you glue the pieces together; then glue them neatly. A thin line of glue spread on both surfaces to be glued is all you need. When you clamp the pieces together, a very small amount of glue should squeeze out of the joint. Some woodworkers tell you to wipe away the glue that squeezes out with a damp rag; if you do that, you are almost certain to see the glue on the project after you finish the project! A better way is to let the glue dry to about the texture of cottage cheese and then pare it off with a sharp chisel. Use the chisel bevel-edge down, as shown in Illus. 9-1; this will prevent it from digging into the wood. After the glue has been removed in this way, a couple of quick passes with a scraper (or with the chisel used as a scraper) will eliminate all traces of the glue. On the other hand, if you let the glue dry completely, removing it is very difficult.

How much sanding you must do depends on the nature of the project. Some experts tell us that we shouldn't sand too much—that is, to the extent that the project starts to disappear. Most rustic-looking projects require less sanding than do projects that are more formal. On all projects we should at least sand the milling marks out of the lumber; this is best done with a belt sander (Illus. 9-2 and 9-3) or a random orbital sander (Illus. 9-4), but it can be done as well by hand. I have found that if you sand the wood *too* smooth (with sandpaper finer than 150 grit), Danish oil finishes or stains don't stick well or evenly because you haven't left pores for them to sink into.

If there are many saw marks in the edge grain

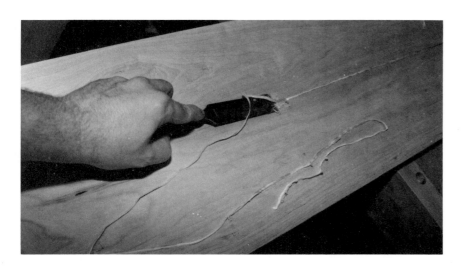

Illus. 9-1. If you remove the squeezed-out glue while it is still the texture of cottage cheese, it will come up neatly, perhaps in a single "string" as shown here.

Illus. 9-2. Use a large-based belt sander or a smaller one with a sanding frame. Very large areas can be sanded very flat with this sander, which has an available sanding frame, shown in Illus. 9-3.

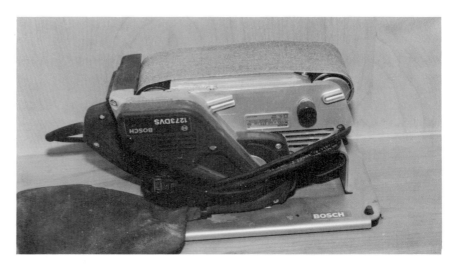

Illus. 9-3. The sanding frame for the sander.

Illus. 9-4. The manufacturers of random orbit sanders claim that these sanders have the speed of belt sanders and produce finishes similar to those produced by pad sanders. While I wouldn't take either part of that claim too seriously, I do find myself using the tool more often, usually with very satisfactory results. Please note that both of the sanders shown here have dust collectors. I wouldn't buy any kind of sander without a dust-collection attachment.

of the wood, they should be sanded out as well; for sanding very curvy edges, use the sanding drums shown in Illus. 9-5; they are inexpensive and readily available at good hardware or hobby stores or by mail from a variety of vendors.

Determining what finish to use on a project is more a matter of choice. For the "natural wood" look, I prefer a penetrating oil finish like Watco® or Minwax®, both available in a fair variety of colors. Both of these finishes are relatively bad smelling, so I prefer to use them only outside, obviously only during warm weather.

In cool weather, I'm more inclined to use a water cleanup product like Hydrocote® polyurethane, which is colorless, odorless, and both quick and easy to use. An excellent way to apply this material is with a rag. Be sure to wear your rubber gloves. I find that I only have to wait half an hour or so for the project to dry enough for a 600-grit sanding; then I quickly wipe it with a damp rag,

and apply another application of the Hydrocote. Regularly, I've applied six or seven coats of the product to the same project in a single day.

To accentuate certain colors in a project, I use acrylic paints with foam brushes for the large areas and then complete the details with artist brushes. Sometimes air-brushing is handy. You are sure to find a finishing method that you'll come to prefer. If it works for you, use it!

Wax can be used at the conclusion of any finishing schedule or alone. Scrub in the wax with steel wool (or preferably one of the nonmetallic equivalents, like those from 3-M), and then remove the excess by buffing the wax with a soft cloth. Do this once a day for a week, once a week for a month, and once a year for eternity. This formula, a holdover from the nineteenth century, is still good advice; old pieces that have lasted have invariably been treated this way.

Illus. 9-5. Drum sanders for hand drills.

10.
Tips for Table Makers and Other Woodworkers

This section contains miscellaneous information on table-making and other areas of woodworking that you may find helpful.

Removing Wood Stains from Your Hands
Hands can become stained from working woods like walnut or cherry, or by woods that are still "green." To remove these stains, first wash your hands, and then try scrubbing them with lemon juice, either fresh squeezed or from concentrate. If lemon juice won't remove that wood stain, it probably won't come out except with the passage of time.

Darkening Cherry Wood
Cherry is a wood that darkens beautifully with age. Sometimes that darkening is uneven, though, for we leave things on our furniture. If you'd like to achieve several years worth of darkening even before you deliver your project, carefully give it a very diluted coating of sodium hydroxide. Sodium hydroxide is not a pigmented stain. Instead, it works by changing the pH of the wood. Sodium hydroxide is most readily available to you as household *lye* or as saw blade cleaner, both caustic alkalines. It doesn't take much to do the job, but you'll have to work quickly and carefully, for lye can dissolve human skin. Also, be aware that sodium hydroxide passes off vapors. Sodium hydroxide doesn't penetrate very deeply, so you'll have to sand off the raised grain very carefully before proceeding with whatever finish you'd apply next.

Painting Carvings
These instructions may prove particularly helpful if you are planning on making the Ducks Unlimited table presented in Chapter 37. When painting a carving, never use a color as it comes from the tube. Always mix colors with other colors to get good effects. Colors mixed in this way are more striking. Second, always paint the black sections of a carving last; then begin to "clean" the brush by rubbing out all possible paint randomly over the entire painted carving. This imparts a "rustic" or "country" look that's sure to improve your project's appearance.

Marking Knife
A sharp, spare plane iron makes an excellent marking knife. Always mark on the pull stroke, using the trailing edge of the plane's edge. The comparatively large back of the plane iron provides a terrific flat bearing surface that is sure to be parallel to what it is being marked against.

Tool Care
Never leave a tool or other object with wooden threads screwed tight when it is not being used. Leave the threads loose, to prevent their being damaged as changes in humidity and atmospheric pressure work against the tightened nut. For sim-

Above: This computer desk remains the centerpiece of my office even a decade after its initial construction. One of the advantages of building your own furniture is that if you are patient enough, you can modify the furniture until it is exactly right for you. Left: This lamp table is proof that a project needn't be made of rare or exotic materials to be quite handsome.

A

Above: A table with an insert top flanked by two comfortable chairs. The close-up below shows the spalted maple top used in this table to create a specific mood. Additionally, tops of bird's-eye maple, Corian®, and matching cherry are available for use with this table. You're sure to be able to devise attractive inserts for use with your own table.

Above: This workbench has a Veritas twin-screw vise
at one end. Right-handed woodworkers should turn
the bench around and mount the "front vise" on the
other side. Right: the low plant table being put to
use.

Above: Peter Mader's handsome harvest table would make an attractive addition to most dining rooms. If your dining room is larger or smaller than Peter Mader's dining room shown here, you can easily adjust the size of the table as described in Chapter 20. Left: This decorative planter is an excellent project for a beginning woodworker. I built the one shown here over 20 years ago.

Right: a close-up of Bob Ayers' "Ducks Unlimited" table.

Left and below: A close-up of the displays carved into the top of the "Ducks Unlimited" table. Your table may feature details other than the hunting motif carved in Ayers' table. Mine will feature antique woodworking hand tools with shavings instead of the dried flowers shown here.

E

Designer kitchen table.

Using commercial Queen Anne legs on this table makes its construction far simpler than one might initially believe.

Dr. Roholt's pine burl tables are every bit as artistic as they are functional.

F

Below: All of the flat stock in this gate-leg table is plywood. Built in the very early 1900's, this table may change your attitude about the appropriate use of plywood.

Above: I can't imagine having a kitchen that doesn't have room for a rolling work station like this butcher block table. At least 500 very large batches of bagels have been made on this table over the dozen years of its existence.

The gate-leg table with its leaves extended.

This simple kitchen table can be built in a weekend.

Your hobby table is very likely to be used as much as this one is. There was virtually no possibility of removing all the items stocked on it to get a "clear" photo of it; this has got to speak well for its practicality.

ilar reasons, router bits should be removed from the router's collet after you have finished with them; having the bits rust in the collets, and having the collet threads stick together, perhaps only from the resins deposited there in the routing process, can freeze up a collet so that only a trip to a repair station can correct things.

Sprung Joints

This tip is particularly useful to woodworkers who set up their jointers so quickly that the boards they wish to glue up sometimes have "snips" at their ends. The joint in a glued panel will dry out nearest the ends first. If we glue up stock that is slightly sniped (worst case) or exactly flat, sooner or later the boards are sure to dry out, and the joints will begin to come apart at the seams. Springing the joint forestalls the panel's eventual destruction. The "sprung" joint has a gap of, say, one fine shaving running all but the first and last few inches of a joint; this gap is "sprung" under clamping pressure, and as the ends of the board dry out and shrink over time, panels so made have much less tendency to come apart at the glue joints. When a sprung joint is used, the material dries out and the ends start to shrink; they won't come unglued. I suppose a really careful worker could spring his joints on the jointer or with a regular bench plane. For me, the only possible tool for this job is the Lie-Nielsen reproduction of the Stanley #95 plane. I use this elegant tool to "spring" joints on stock that is no thicker than $7/8''$, as is nearly all the panel stock in our shops.

Working Effectively with Plywood

Following is advice on how to work with plywood:

1. Use masking tape on the lines you're cutting, to prevent the plywood from splintering.

2. Run screws into dowels planted at cross angles rather than trying to drive them into end grain, where they have no chance of sticking.

3. Use a second sheet of plywood as a rip guide when no long straightedge is available.

4. In many applications, it's possible to finish a sheet before cutting it; do this to save quite a bit of time.

5. Break edges by running sandpaper from the inner portion of the plywood sheet outwards to the open edge.

6. Always use backups to prevent tear-out when drilling.

Applying Glue to Large, Flat Areas

If you're applying glue to fairly large, flat areas, a paint roller half the width of the area will do a faster, neater, and more economical job. Keep the glue in a roller pan, and roll it on as needed. Between (fairly frequent) uses, cover the pan and the roller with generous amounts of clear self-adhesive plastic to keep the glue fresh and workable.

Cutting Plugs

Here's an easy way to cut plugs: First, cut the plugs in neat rows with your plug cutter and your drill press. Then put a strip of tape across the drilled side. Use your table saw or band saw to saw off the other side; the tape will keep the plugs from flying around the saw in a potentially dangerous manner. When you remove the scrap stock, the plugs will stick to the piece of tape, making them far more convenient to use.

Glue Blocks

For centuries, glue blocks have been used to strengthen woodworking joints. For some reason, they have gone out of fashion. One of the things this means is that woodworkers are more frequently called upon to repair the work of others. When some joints have come unglued, but you can't reglue the entire joint, you can add glue blocks. If the joints can be drawn tight even though they can't be disassembled, you can again use glue blocks to repair them. Clamp the carcass together the way it was supposed to be, and apply several sizeable glue blocks with hide glue similar to what the original maker of the piece no doubt should have used. Not only are they good for reinforcing joints in repair work, but they also strengthen joints in out-of-the-way parts of new work.

The best way to get glue blocks is probably to make them of scrap stock; I regularly make strips $3/4''$ x $3/4''$ + the hypotenuse from routine shop rippings that might otherwise just feed the fireplace; I set these in a corner for cutting glue blocks of whatever length a project requires. Using them doesn't take much extra time, and they help to make our assemblies more rigid. Glue blocks have unnecessarily gone out of fashion. It's time we brought them back.

Taper Jig

Here is the ideal jig for the quick occasional or odd-angle taper that your regular taper jig won't accommodate (Illus. 10-1). Cut an appropriate notch in the end of a suitably wide board with a band saw. If you have to cut lots of tapered pieces, mount a clamp to the board to help ensure that

Illus. 10-1. A simple taper jig that can be quickly made. Draw the taper on the piece to be tapered. Set the piece to be tapered over the edge so the lines you draw intersect with the edges of the jig. Trace the overlap, and then cut it out. One way to cut it out is with a band saw. If it is a size you use frequently, save it and use it to cut repetitive pieces. Otherwise, use it as scrap stock.

your fingers stay clear of the blade. This taper jig can be planned by sight on the saw table, is quick to make, and is disposable. I was ready to cut tapers less than three minutes after I decided to make a jig to cut them.

Wood Patches

Sawdust-filled epoxy cement makes probably the best of all possible wood patches, especially for use under epoxy or urethane varnishes. This is a most valuable accessory when building things like tool stands which must remain absolutely rigid. When building such an object, use this mixture on all joints generously, but not wastefully.

Wood Filler

Even the best planks you're likely to find will have some minor imperfections in them. As the cost of hardwoods keeps rising, cutting around these minor flaws becomes less and less practical and artful patching becomes more and more desirable. Stick shellac is good, but it's also fragile and never quite the right color, and blending tones can be messy, time-consuming, and not very precise. None of the various putty, wood dough, or "plastic wood" products seem suitable for more than the most ordinary applications; they too have color-matching problems, and, like the shellac sticks, they don't take finish in quite the same way as regular wood. In your workshop, however, you already have the key ingredients to a superior wood-patching compound that will always match your project perfectly, and will always be fresh because you make it up only as you need it. Master carver Chris Effrem showed me how to create this compound he called "**scrape**" a decade ago, and I've used it ever since, never failing to get superior results.

The materials you need to create this compound are extremely simple. Buy a small bottle of liquid hide glue; this works better than the hot hide glue you might make from crystals and water, because it sets rather more slowly. Use hot hide glue for those applications when you're pressed for time. Buy small bottles, so that you work with fresh glue more often. The other ingredient is the cutoff from the board that requires the patch.

Set the cutoff in the vise on your workbench, end-grain up (Illus. 10-2). Put a drop of liquid hide glue on the end grain (Illus. 10-3). With a very sharp chisel, but not one of your best chisels, scrape the end grain, through the glue, in strokes a couple of inches long (Illus. 10-4 and 10-5). Alter the scraping strokes enough to thoroughly mix the fine shavings you raise with the glue. When the mixture of glue and "dust" reaches the texture your experimenting demonstrates to be most use-

ful to you, apply it to the damaged area with the chisel (Illus. 10-6). I find that I get best results when I blend the "scrape" so that it is somewhat thicker than commercial wood dough.

It's important to work neatly; after all, your goal is to repair an imperfection, not to make a mess with glue and dust. After the glue has set, this "scrape" will sand and finish nicely. Hide glue does less to prevent the finish from working invisibly than do the more readily available PVC

Illus. 10-2. The glue, the chisel, and the scrap of wood already positioned in the vise.

Illus. 10-4 and 10-5. Scrape the end grain through the glue until you have a fine paste on the end of the chisel.

Illus. 10-3. Put a single drop of liquid hide glue on the end grain.

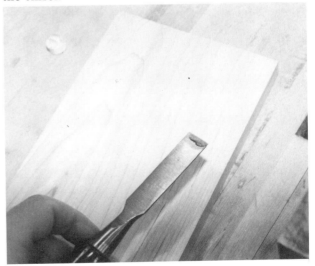

Illus. 10-5.

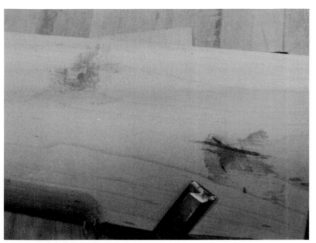

Illus. 10-6. Apply the glue to the afflicted area with a chisel.

woodworking glues. Some woodworkers prefer epoxy-type adhesives.

Some woodworkers make repairs of this type with white glue and the contents of their belt sander's dust bag. Don't use these materials for other than the crudest work; the dust in your belt sander's bag includes small abrasive particles which are certain to ruin your finish, and, unless your cleanup is absolutely meticulous, the white glue is sure to show up under almost any finish. Besides, the micro-thin "scraped" shavings are the perfect consistency for this application.

If you must use a plank other than a disposable cutoff, be certain to clean the end off, or to cut off enough so the piece isn't out of square when you get ready to use it in a project. This step is almost as important as cleaning and lightly oiling or waxing the chisel. Cleaning up the plank and the tool while the material is wet is much easier than chipping off dried glue.

This is a useful technique for patching inexpensively. Even if you have a satisfactory method for doing this, this one is worth experimenting with: There's no telling when having another technique like this will save your project.

Buying Stock

Get to know your lumber merchant, and always insist on top-quality stock. It's worth paying a bit more for quality timber. I recently bought 100 board feet of 1″ rough cherry, paying perhaps 25 percent higher than I would normally pay for poorer-quality wood—though I think the premium material I was working was well worth the extra cost. The whole stack was as flat as the pair of pieces I used for the table's top. I took out two pieces, 1″ x 8″ x 8′, and cut them to lengths of about 74″ with my sabre saw. Then I jointed one edge of each clean in a single pass. Next, I jointed one face of each clean in a single pass. Then I sawed each to 7⁹/₁₆″, so I'd have a bit to joint off, and still have my desired 15″ panel from two boards. I set the surfacer to 1″; two passes made each board perfectly clean at ¹⁵/₁₆″. Then I took it down to ¾″, not because I had to, but because that was what the project dictated. Using the best lumber I could find helped me to get clean, flat lumber very quickly.

Tables

11.
Workbench

The workbench may be the most important table you build. A good one will make it easier to build all the other tables in this book. Now, even as some professional woodworkers criticize the old-fashioned workbench, it is undergoing some modernization and is becoming an even more useful part of the shop, particularly because the finest detail work is still done by hand.

One indication that woodworkers are interested in the topic of workbenches is that whole books

Parts List for the Workbench

Label	Part	Quantity	Thickness	Width	Length
A	Top	1	2″	18½″	75½″
B	Top Sides	2	2″	4¼″	75½″
C	Legs	4	2″	3½″	36″
D	Tops and bottoms	4	2″	2½″	18½″
E	Stretchers	2	2″	4″	48″
F	End Stretchers	2	2″	2½″	12″
G	Vise Part	1	2″	6″	22½″
H	Vise part	1	2″	8″	22½″
I	Bolts for stretchers	4			
J	Lag screws for Jorgensen vise	2			
K	Jorgensen #40709 vise	1			
L	Veritas twin-screw vise	1			

Illus. 11-1. A workbench for
left-handed woodworkers. Make
yours a mirror image of this if
you are right-handed. Also see
page C of the color section.

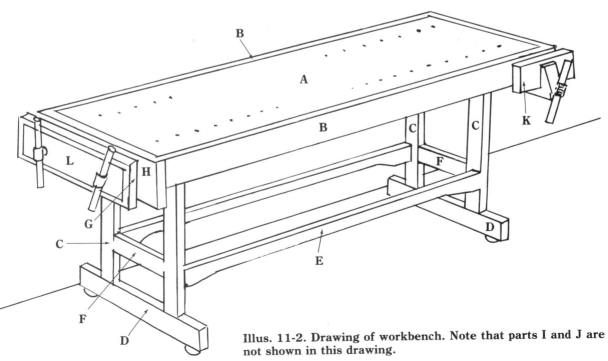

Illus. 11-2. Drawing of workbench. Note that parts I and J are
not shown in this drawing.

and magazines are devoted to them. There are so many varieties of workbenches that nearly all serious woodworkers seem to believe themselves in possession of the "ideal" one.

My first real bench was patterned after one built by Tage Frid, which appeared in the fall, 1976 issue of *Fine Woodworking*, although mine was somewhat heavier and higher than his, and was made to be the mirror image of his. His was made for a right-handed woodworker, and I am left-handed. It's important that one be planing into the bench rather than just into the tail vise, and it's important to be able to work around the project in the "head" vise. While the vise on this original bench has served me well for over 15 years, I decided that I needed a bigger bench. Even before it was finished, the bigger bench was cut back apart and rebuilt to accommodate the Veritas twin-screw vise. Coupling this vise with a Jorgensen 40709 Rapid Action Woodworker's Vise gives me terrific clamping versatility. When I use this bench with my Frid-style bench I'm able to use four different kinds of vise.

Building Instructions

Mortise-and-tenon and glue the legs into the top and bottom bases, and mortise-and-tenon and glue the end stretchers into the legs (Illus. 11-3 and 11-4). Add cross dowels to the tenons, for

Illus. 11-4. Clean up the tenons with a plane.

strength. Mount the long stretchers with through bolts and nuts (Illus. 11-5–11-8), in case you have to move the workbench a long distance (Illus. 11-9) and want to move it flat. I discovered the first time I swept around the bench with a broom that I had mounted the stretchers too low, so I wound up taking them out and cutting an arc in each piece to permit space for the bench. If you don't want to perform this extra step, be sure to mount your stretchers at least a couple of inches higher than suggested.

Illus. 11-3. Drill the mortises, and then clean them up with a chisel.

Illus. 11-5. Drilling holes for the long bolts in the stretchers.

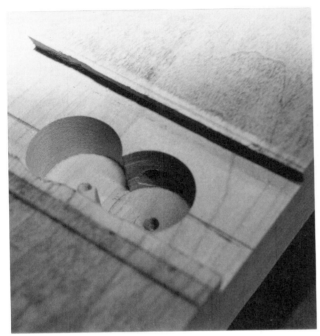

Illus. 11-6. Drilling the other direction for this joint; if you haven't drilled very straight, you may have to drill a second hole.

Illus. 11-7. The bolt with washers ready to accept the nut.

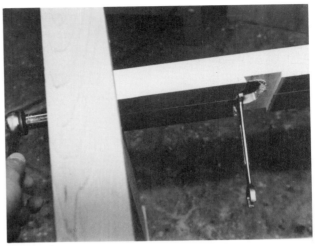

Illus. 11-8. Attaching the two ends of the bolt through the leg/stretcher assembly.

Illus. 11-9. I prefer to add steel-tipped furniture feet to benches that are likely to be slid around the shop on occasion.

Glue the side rails to the center top, using biscuits for alignment (Illus. 11-10). Cut a notch from one end of the front of the top's side rail, and add a spacer behind it so that the Jorgensen vise can be mounted (Illus. 11-11).

Note that it may be difficult to align the parts. While biscuits may allow ¼″ or so of lateral movement, I had no chance of moving the rear apron ⅛″ and the front apron 1/32″ in the opposite direction with my mallet. So, I laid the rear jaw piece of the Veritas vise over the end of the bench, and traced the shapes of the parts. Then I used the micro-adjuster feature on the new Bosch router to make the rear jaw fit flush to the tabletop (Illus. 11-12 and 11-13).

To mount the vise, first remove the cotter pin from the back end of the guide rod and note the position of the roller nut; then slide the front-jaw assembly out of the vise (Illus. 11-14 and 11-15). Attach the back part of the jaw to the bottom of the bench with a pair of lag screws, and mount the front of the vise to the front edge of the top with #14 x 2″ wood screws. Reinstall the front-jaw assembly and the roller nut and close the vise; as soon as you replace the cotter pin (Illus. 11-16), the vise is ready to use (Illus. 11-17). Some woodworkers might set the front of the vise into the table far enough that a wooden insert can be added to bring it flush, and add another wooden jaw to the front vise portion as well. I haven't done either of these steps, figuring that I will remember to add pieces of scrap stock when I put delicate work in the vise. This useful American-made vise is very easy to install.

The Veritas vise is not as easy to install. It comes with six pages of instructions which must be followed precisely for the vise to work properly. Several months after I received my vise, I received

Illus. 11-10. A view of the biscuits and glue used to mount the top's side rails; this is probably why the pieces wouldn't slip back and forth for perfect alignment.

Illus. 11-11. Clamp a spacer in place for the Jorgensen vise to mount to.

Illus. 11-12. A view of the Bosch micro-adjuster router, one of the most desirable routers on the market.

Illus. 11-13. The Bosch router made it possible to fit the end of the bench, even though it was less than perfect.

Illus. 11-14. The Jorgensen vise ready to be attached to the bench.

Illus. 11-15. Keep the nut aligned on the vise so that it will work freely.

Illus. 11-16 (above). A view of
the Jorgensen cotter pin; with it
in place, the front vise cannot be
removed. Illus. 11-17 (right).
The Jorgensen vise installed—
with the bench still upside-down.

a five-page questionnaire about the assembly procedure; apparently there have been quite a few
people who haven't followed the directions. Please
follow the printed instructions *exactly* rather than
trying to improvise the installation.

The jaw pieces on the Veritas vise should be
2″ thick, and wide enough to cover the entire rear
jaw of the vise. After determining how far apart
you want the jaws to be, drill two holes in each of
the wooden vise parts you have made with a 1½″
bit (Illus. 11-18); then, in the rear jaw drill a pair
of ⅜″ holes for the screw saver pins (the pins
which prevent the work being held in the vise from
riding on the threaded screw which operates the

vise). Next, drill matching ½″ holes in the front
jaw so the vise may be closed over these protec-
tors. Attach the rear vise part to the bench using
the hex bolt and round nut provided. I found this
to be the hardest part of the installation; working
by eye, I didn't line up all these long drillings as
precisely as they should have been aligned. This
was complicated by the fact that the directions
called for drilling with some drill sizes that even
my very well-equipped shop did not have; I chose
the closest larger size, with less than sterling results! Because of the combination of errors, it took
me 40 minutes to install these important parts.

Illus. 11-18. Drilling to attach the 1½″ nuts to the
underside of the bench.

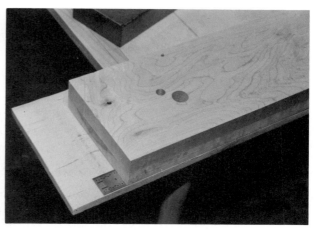

Illus. 11-19. Note the ruler being used as a carrier
to taper the bottom of the face jaw so it is thinner
than the top.

The directions for the Veritas vise say to taper the front jaw of the vise; use a flat board or a piece of plywood as a carrier (Illus. 11-19). Set a thin piece at the edge, and then set the piece to be tapered on it (Illus. 11-20). Take two very small passes to achieve the desired thickness.

Attaching the chain and the front vise jaws to the bench is easy, though, and the vise is extremely useful (Illus. 11-21 and 11-22). It will put even pressure on both sides of even a wide, long panel while you are working on it. The capacity of this bench has to be in excess of seven feet. The excellent Veritas manual even gives directions for installing a speed knob on the handle; I will be doing this soon.

After installing the vise, I drilled thirty-two ¾" holes at close intervals all along the front and back edges of the table. Bench dogs will ride in these 4¼"-deep holes (Illus. 11-23 and 11-24). I will generally be using wooden dogs to protect planes and other tools that might come in contact with them. I found a common hardware-store ¾" spade bit to work far better and less expensively than the bit recommended by the manufacturer (Illus. 11-25 and 11-26).

One quick note about adding a finish to the bench: Sand the bench top with a large sander until it is perfectly flat (Illus. 11-27). A couple of good coats of boiled linseed oil makes an effective finish.

Other additions that will happen soon to the bench shown include tool storage underneath; that

Illus. 11-20. Gluing up the face jaw of the Veritas twin-screw vise.

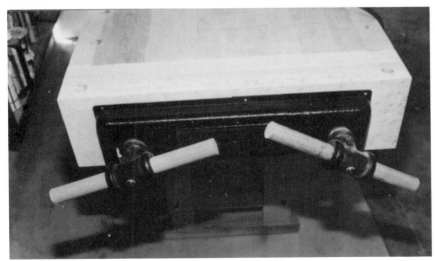

Illus. 11-21. The installed twin-screw vise.

Illus. 11-22. Inside the twin-screw vise is a pair of heavy posts that keep the woodworking project off the vise screws.

Illus. 11-23 and 11-24. The Veritas hold-fast works in the bench-dog holes, whereas the old-style hold-fasts require a collar (like the one shown in Illus. 11-24) for mounting.

Illus. 11-24.

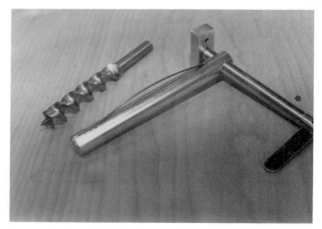

Illus. 11-25. The Veritas Wonder-Dog and the drill recommended by Veritas.

Illus. 11-26. It was easier to drill the dog holes in the top with the spade bit than with either of the alternatives—even though the bit overheated and broke on the very last hole.

is part of the motivation for matching the heights of the stretcher all the way around the bench. I haven't yet determined whether this will consist of just a shelf, a 16″ x 46½″ removable tray, or a series of drawers for different types of tools (Illus. 11-28).

Whatever happens below the bench, I can tell already that this bench's top will see a great deal of use (Illus. 11-29).

Illus. 11-27. Sand the tabletop with a large sander until it is perfectly flat before you apply any finish; a couple of good coats of boiled linseed oil will leave a repairable finish that will protect the bench well.

Illus. 11-28. A couple of racks for mounting clamps will make a handy addition to any bench. This helps to keep the clamps where you're most likely to use them.

Illus. 11-29. As these two workbenches demonstrate, you will probably put your workbench to extensive use. Try not to leave your woodworking tools and equipment on your workbench, as was done here.

12.
Hobby Table

This table (Illus. 12-1 and 12-2) was built to the specifications of my son-in-law, an avid model builder. He needed a portable table and a couple of specifically placed indentations for placement of parts of the model builder's tool kit.

To achieve portability, I used Gerber® legs, readily available in hardware stores everywhere, which screw into base plates which are, in turn, screwed to the underside of the tabletop (Illus. 12-3). By nature of the design of the legs, these tables are slightly less stable than their aproned counterparts. The legs are also somewhat more expensive than one might pay to build the table from scratch; for those two reasons, I would not make these legs my first choice. On the other hand, all you need to install them is a screwdriver. It is possible, after all, to go into a home center and to buy a piece of very nice plywood or even glued-up hardwood cut to almost any size; then it would be a simple matter of screwing four base

Illus. 12-1. Hobby table. See the parts list and the drawing on the following page and page H of the color section.

Parts List for the Hobby Table

Label	Part	Quantity	Thickness	Width	Length
A	Top	1	¾″	24″	30″
B	Leg	4	*		27″
C	Drawer Front	1	¾″	4″	10″
	Drawer Hanger	2	¾″	4″	12″
	Drawer Sides	2	¾″	4″	12″
	Drawer Back	1	⅛″	9½″	11½″

*1¾″ taper to 1″ diameter

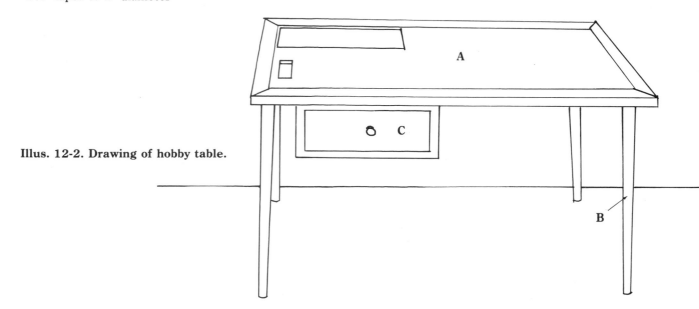

Illus. 12-2. Drawing of hobby table.

Illus. 12-3. These Gerber legs will be fastened into a base plate that permits straight or angled mounting.

plates onto the underside of the top (Illus. 12-4) and turning the legs into them (Illus. 12-5). One might conceivably have a table in five minutes.

Illus. 12-4. Mark the corners and screw the base plate to the underside of the top.

Illus. 12-5. Here's how the legs look both straight and angled.

I wanted something slightly fancier than a piece of plywood for this top, so I edged the piece with mitred pieces of matching wood. While I biscuited the work to align the edge pieces to the piece of particleboard which was the main table, I also clamped the corners flat after I was sure they had been properly aligned (Illus. 12-6).

Illus. 12-6. After the edging has been glued and clamped to the top, clamp the corners in the other direction, to ensure that they meet flush.

Check, double-check and recheck settings as you rout the slots for a tool or parts box (Illus. 12-7–12-9). Be sure to measure this to fit *your* tool box rather than the one that fits on the table illustrated here.

Rout all the corners of these "slots" round; square them up with as wide a chisel as you have (Illus. 12-10). Make these chisel cuts cross-grain before you make them long-grain.

To make the drawers, plane the stock to size. Cut notches for the sides. Glue and clamp them.

Nail the drawer sides into the rabbets on the front edge (Illus. 12-11). The back can be fitted the same way. Add a handle of choice, and the project is ready for use.

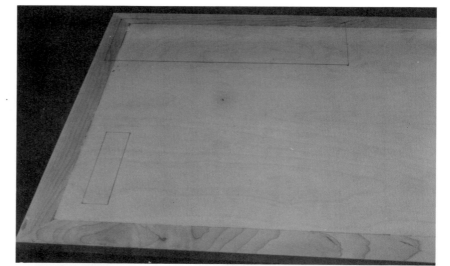

Illus. 12-7. The layout for the top grooves.

Illus. 12-8. The big slot has been cut, and the smaller one is being prepared.

Illus. 12-9. A close-up of the router guide.

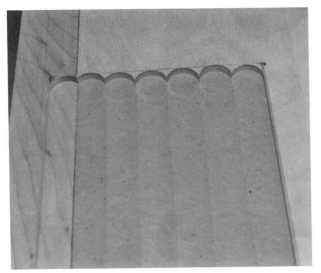

Illus. 12-10. Is it quicker to remove these corners with a router or with a chisel? I opted for a chisel.

Illus. 12-11. A view of how the drawer works.

13.
Practical Work Desk

A useful desk has to provide both a large work area and adequate storage space. That it be relatively inexpensive and portable would be a real bonus. Here's a simple desk (Illus. 13-1 and 13-2) that meets all these requirements. Indeed, this is a desk that's so simple that few woodworking/homeowner publications would even consider mentioning it.

Start with two 2-drawer filing cabinets. Filing cabinets come in a variety of sizes and qualities; since this will be a very inexpensive desk, use top-quality filing cabinets. Basically, they come in "letter" and "legal" widths; the "legal"-size cabinets are about 3″ wider. They come in a variety of depths: I have seen inexpensive cabinets that were 20″ deep, moderate cabinets that were 24″ deep, and high-quality cabinets 28″ deep. I bought Invincible® 28″ letter-width cabinets; the store had an unmatched pair in stock, and I wasn't terribly concerned about color.

Illus. 13-1. This desk can provide useful work space.

Parts List for the Practical Work Desk

Label	Part	Quantity	Thickness	Width	Length
A	Top*	1			
B	Filing Cabinet**	4			

*Interior or exterior solid-core top. Interior tops (doors) are commonly 1½″ thick, 32″ wide, and 78″ long. Exterior tops are commonly 1¾″ thick, 32″ wide, and 78″ long.

**I prefer Invincible® two-drawer, deep units.

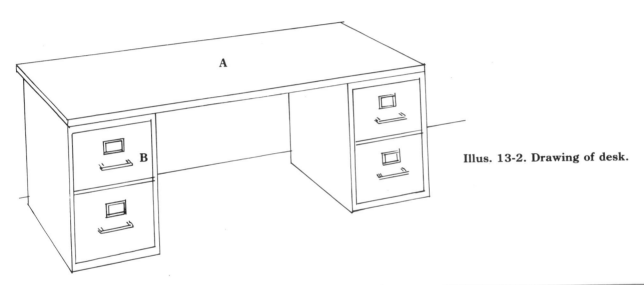

Illus. 13-2. Drawing of desk.

Ensure that the cabinets sit level on the floor. As Illus. 13-3 indicates, I had to do a bit of shimming to make the cabinets level on the floor of my basement office. First, I put a piece of 2″-wide material of the proper thickness in the front of the cabinet; this piece was nearly ¾″ thick. After it was in place, cutting the tapers for the sides wasn't really a problem. Since both cabinets had to be shimmed, I make sure that they were plumb after the shimming.

To complete the desk, attach a flush door over the filing cabinets. A standard 32″ x 80″ door (Illus. 13-4) is perfect for this application. Solid-core doors might work better in the long run than hollow-core doors, but your choice may be dictated by cost. Doors generally come made of birch, luan, or ash. Ash doors are currently considered the

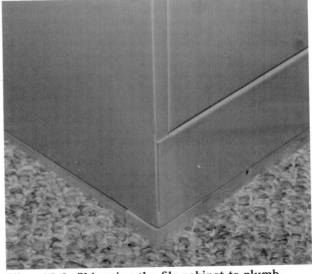

Illus. 13-3. Shimming the file cabinet to plumb.

Illus. 13-4. Note the amount of overhang that this 32″ door has over these 28″ file cabinets; if you use cabinets with less depth, you'll want to move them forward, so the overhang doesn't much exceed the amount shown here.

most attractive. But their porous, open-grained surfaces make finishing them more difficult, for they have to be "filled" with paste wood filler to make them flat enough to write on. This paste filler is painted on with a brush, and then is rubbed off across the grain to fill the pores; after drying and a good sanding, the material is ready for staining and/or varnishing.

I prefer the appearance of birch doors; varnished, they are a pleasing amber color with very little grain. Luan doors seem too soft (and, to me, too "cheap" looking) to use as writing surfaces.

As the cost of doors has risen, there seems to be another quite acceptable alternative. Find a used door, prepare its surface, and apply a plastic laminate coating—like Formica®. I paid only $3 for the door that's on my desk. I bought a 36″ by 96″ sheet of Surf-colored Formica for just over $2 per square foot, and used less than a pint of water-based contact cement. The total cost was approximately $50, and the resulting desk top is a joy to work at. The laminating process is described in depth in the next section.

If you find that the desk top slides around too much on the filing cabinets, put a bit of thin-foam packing material on each cabinet before setting the door in place; this will stop all movement. This may be particularly useful if the desk isn't bounded on at least two sides by a wall.

Since the work surface is a little high at 31⅜″, I often use a stool when I work at this desk.

Installing Plastic Laminate

Illus. 13-5–13-30 show plastic being put on the door described in this chapter. It was applied by a friend who happens to be an expert laminate installer in his shop. Formica® plastic laminate was used. We used his glue from a five-gallon-pail, and "cut-off" material of a similar color to "seal" the bottom. He applied the contact cement with a "throwaway" paint roller and an aluminum-foil-lined painting pan. By storing the roller in a plastic bag between jobs and pouring the excess cement back into the five-gallon-pail, he managed to install the laminate quite economically. Since this paint roller and a J-roller are the only equipment you need, this is a practical home-shop project.

It is worthwhile to mention one technique not illustrated in this chapter: If an edge comes loose while you're filing, a good whack with a mallet may force it to stay in place; similarly, a good squeeze in a clamp will provide far more pressure than you can provide with a J-roller, so it may be just the thing to "set" a reluctant corner in place.

Overall, the laminating process is so simple that after you have experienced it, you're likely to use laminates often in projects where they might be appropriate. And not only is laminating easy, but it is also quick.

We spent about three hours laminating the door, but most of that time was spent doing other things in the shop not involved with the actual laminating job. If it takes you a bit longer in your own shop, especially in the learning stages, that shouldn't be a problem. Many times professionals will coat a pair of surfaces before they go home for the evening, and then assemble them when they come to work the next day. How could working with material this forgiving be a problem?

Illus. 13-5. The cut-off pieces of laminate can be coated with contact cement even while stacked on one another.

Illus. 13-7. While we waited for the cement to dry, we cut some narrow strips off the piece of laminate; these will be used for the edges.

Illus. 13-6. Then the entire door surface is coated; the contact cement goes on colored (usually green), and is ready to be joined when it has dried to a clear color.

Illus. 13-8. The excess length is being cut from the laminate.

Illus. 13-9. The cut-off end has two narrow strips cut from it, but there is still a fair amount of waste. You may be able to visit an installer and find enough "waste" to laminate a number of small projects.

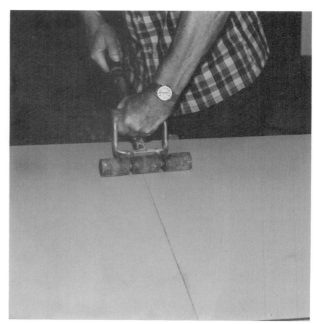

Illus. 13-11. Use a roller on the laminate pieces after they have been cemented in place.

Illus. 13-10. After the cement has dried, set the pieces on the bottom.

Illus. 13-12. Two types of roller. One might initially think the one on the left would apply more pressure, but this isn't so. A person can only generate so much pressure, and the J roller on the right concentrates the pressure over fewer square inches than does the one on the left.

Illus. 13-13. If you find that the J roller fills up with cement, you can clean it quite nicely on a disc grinder. The trick is to find the right spot on your grinder so the roller spins slowly enough for the cement to come off. Certainly, anyone who uses a roller to apply material over contact cement will find this preferable to replacing rollers.

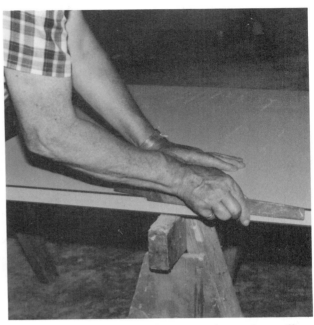

Illus. 13-15. With a file, clean the sharp edges off the laminate.

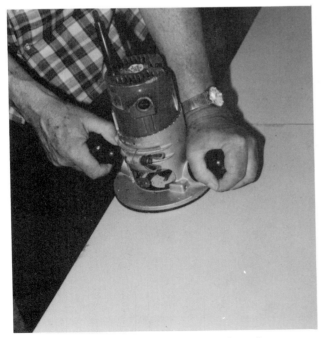

Illus. 13-14. After the bottom pieces have been cemented in place, the excess material is removed with a router and a flush trim bit.

Illus. 13-16. After putting cement on the remaining pieces and the edges and letting it dry, apply first the end caps.

Illus. 13-17. Use a roller to put the end caps in place.

Illus. 13-19. After flush trimming, file the edges at about this angle (which is roughly 5°), to remove any possibility of snags.

Illus. 13-18. Rout the excess material off the ends.

Illus. 13-20. Use the file card on the file about midway through the job, to keep the file cutting smoothly.

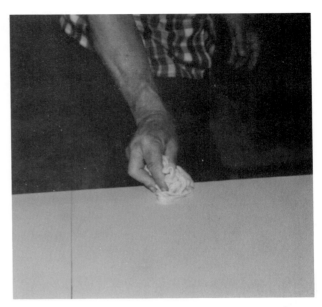

Illus. 13-21. Apply the long strips to the sides of the door, and rout the material to size and file it to fit; when this step has been completed, you will have covered five of the door's six edges.

Illus. 13-22. With some solvent, wipe any remaining glue off the bottom laminate. Carefully applying Vaseline or Lami-Lube (available where you buy your laminate) to your laminate's surface will permit you to peel the excess material off without having to use solvent.

Illus. 13-23 (above left). Rout the sides and ends flush to what will be the top of the desk. Then apply cement to the top. Illus. 13-24 (above right). After the cement on the top has dried, lay some strips of uncemented laminate loosely on the top; if you don't have laminate, almost any other light, thin material will work. Next, lay the cemented laminate which is to be your tabletop on top of these pieces.

Illus. 13-25. After the top is properly positioned, pull the pieces out.

Illus. 13-26. Use a roller to position the top laminate into place.

Illus. 13-27. Use a router bit with a good bearing to trim the top to fit.

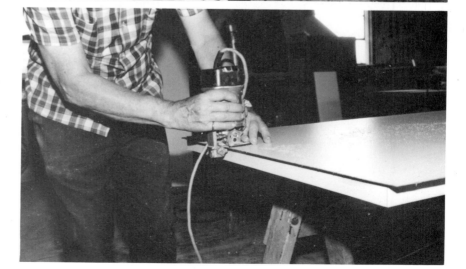

Illus. 13-28 (above left). File the top's edges so there are no sharp edges or burrs. Note the proper angle at both ends of the stroke. Illus. 13-29 (above right). Note the white line between the cement and the black line, which is the actual edge. When this line appears, you know that you have filed just enough. After wiping off any excess cement with solvent, you have completed the lamination.

Illus. 13-30. There are always pieces of laminate like this left over—just enough for small projects. Laminating is so easy that you may well find yourself laminating many projects.

14.
Computer Desk

I became interested in computer furniture after I learned how much easier word processing is than typing, and after I bought my computer. When I saw how poorly made most computer furniture is, especially relative to its price, it seemed that if I could build a line of attractive, economical, custom-built computer furniture, I would have an unending supply of customers. Even though the design of the computer desk described and illustrated in this chapter (Illus. 14-1–14-6) was good enough to be shown in *Fine Woodworking Design Book Four*, the unending stream of customers hasn't appeared. Yet, this desk is extremely appealing because it is simple and adaptable. It is also relatively inexpensive to build. The materials for the cherry computer desk featured here cost approximately $200. This included all wood, adhesives, abrasives, and finishing material.

Because this is a fairly large project, it is broken down into subunits. The rationale for this is not only to organize the work, but also to permit the builder to utilize only those features desired.

It is useful here to consider some background about this desk before delving into the plan. First,

Parts List for Computer Desk
Frame
Four 2″ x 2″ x 28¼″ legs
Four 2″ x 2″ x 24″ cross braces
Two 2″ x 2″ x 58″ long braces

Top
One 1″ x 26″ x 60″ work surface
Two 1″ x 2″ x 26½″ aprons
Two 1″ x 2″ x 60″ aprons

Computer Drawer Unit
Two 1″ x 18½″ x 16″ sides
Two 1″ x 2″ x 23¾″ bottom stretchers
One 1″ x 18½″ x 23¼″ shelf insert
Two 1″ x 2″ x 18½″ mounting strips

Drawer
One 1″ x 7⅛″ x 22″ front
Two 1″ x 6″ x 18½″ sides
One 1″ x 6¼″ x 20¼″ back
One 1″ x 17″ x 20¼″ bottom (Masonite?)

Keyboard Tray
One 1″ x 1″ x 23½″ front
Two 1″ x 2″ x 18½″ sides
Two 1″ x 2″ x 23½″ backs
One ¼″ x 23¼″ x 10″ bottom

Bridge
Two 1½″ x 7¾″ x 14½″ sides
One 1″ x 15″ x 40″ top
Two 1″ x 1½″ x 15″ trim
Two 1″ x 1½″ x 8′ trim

Hardware
Two ¼″ x 2″ x 24″ corks
One drawer glide
One pencil drawer slide
Four feet
Miscellaneous screws

Note: The 1″ thickness for many of the parts of this desk is a nominal thickness; except for the work surface, ¾″ is the exact thickness of all 1″ parts.

Illus. 14-1. Computer desk. Also see page A of the color section.

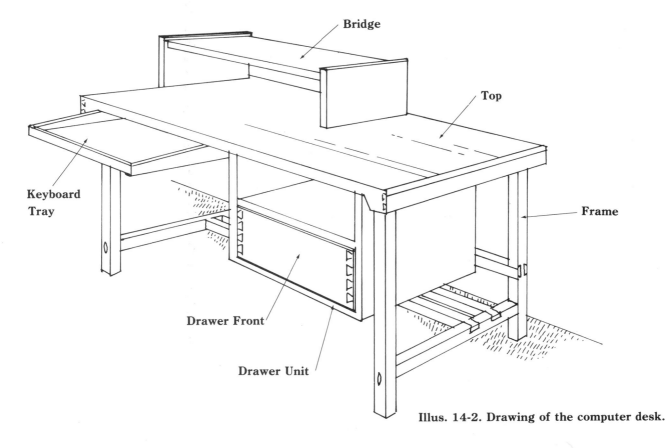

Illus. 14-2. Drawing of the computer desk.

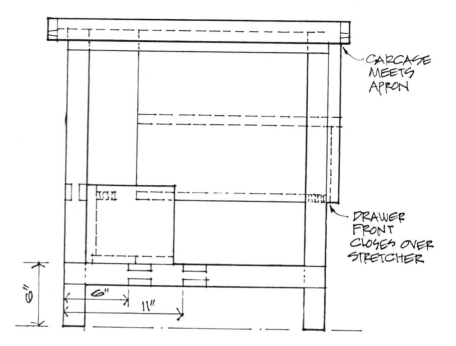

Illus. 14-3. Side view of desk.

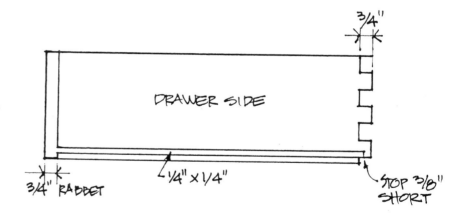

Illus. 14-4. Side view of drawer.

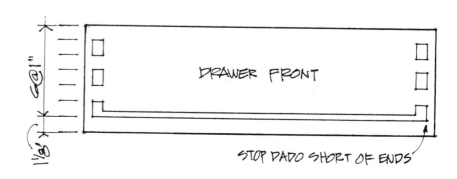

Illus. 14-5. Inside view of the drawer front. The stop dado is just a dado, but the three rectangles on either side indicate through holes, through which the drawer sides fit.

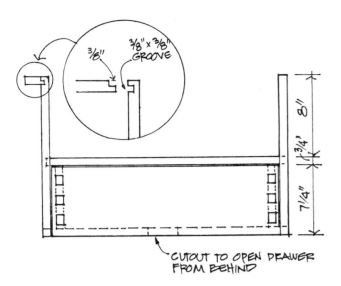

Illus. 14-6. Front view of drawer and computer unit.

this desk was built for a very small work area (my writing room is only roughly six x eight feet); all your measurements should be subject to your (clients') needs. A larger desk will also work well; this desk's size causes me to do all too much of my "desk work" at the dining room table. Second, this desk was made specifically for an IBM-PC computer; if you are building it for another computer, check its dimensions very carefully; at the conclusion of this chapter I offer some suggestions towards modification. Many of the features of this desk were added after the basic unit was in place in my office, and they now seem so logical that I wonder how I could have built the desk without them.

The first thing to make is the frame. After your 2 x 2s have been milled and cut to rough size, cut four 2 x 2 x 28″ legs and four 2 x 2 x 24″ cross braces. Cut "through" mortise-and-tenon joints for the cross braces; or, if you prefer, use bridle joints or dovetails, which look and work as well. Use the joint here that you feel most comfortable with—or which your client prefers. The cross braces go at the top and 6″ from the floor.

Before gluing these leg units together, cut the

joints for the long braces; I used "lap" dovetails (Illus. 14-7), but bridle joints or mortise-and-tenon joints would work as well. Glue up the frame after all parts have been "dry" fit and sanded through 150-grit sandpaper. After the glue has set, clean up any glue dribble and break the edges. At this time, apply the feet, to prevent possible damage while sliding the base around in your workshop.

Illus. 14-7. Half-lapped dovetail joints give the base strength. Note the line where the colors change; the lighter part is normally covered with a drop-in shelf.

Now that your base is ready, prepare the top. Glue up your hardwood (or cut plywood) to 26 x 60″. Cut a rabbet in the apron pieces that is as wide as the top is thick; dovetail the apron pieces together so that the top may be dropped into the rabbet that you have formed. It would be easier and a lot less time-consuming, I suppose, to mitre the apron together; this is a question of style that you will answer when you reach this step. Before you glue the top and the apron together, you should cut a 1″-wide strip out of the front side of the top that is the width of the frame; this will ensure access to the computer in its shelf and to the keyboard which will be on a sliding tray.

Sometime after building the desk, I added a lower shelf to house a new, much larger computer. If the computer shelf in the original plan was 2″ higher, this less attractive addition wouldn't be needed (Illus. 14-8 and 14-9).

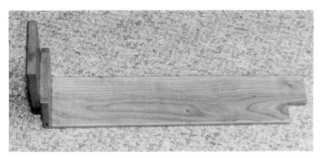

Illus. 14-8. A view of the adapter added to the computer desk some time after it was built. If I had instead built an extra 2″ where the computer originally sat, I would have solved the design problem.

Illus. 14-9. The computer desk with the adapter in place. The author believes both the appearance and the function of the unit have been compromised.

After the top has been glued to the apron, it can be affixed to the stand. I covered the top of the stand with ¼″ cork to absorb shock, and screwed the top onto the legs from the underside.

The next step is to assemble the unit which will house the computer and the drawer for the diskettes. Cut two 18½″ wide by 16″ long sides (or 18″-long sides if you're building to house a more-modern, full-size computer), a 18½″ x 23¼″ shelf insert, and a pair of 2″ x 23¾″ bottom stretchers. Dovetail the stretchers to the sides. Rout dadoes in the sides for the shelf; I did not want the dadoes to extend through the front, so I notched the corners of the shelf to fit the opening.

The drawer for the diskettes (Illus. 14-10) must be at least 6″ deep, if you are storing 5¼″ diskettes. Since the standard size for diskettes seems to be changing to 3½″, a 4″-deep drawer might be satisfactory. Another option is to store the smaller diskettes in a new set of dividers (Illus. 14-11). This is an ideal place to use the diskette organizer idea that was the first item in this series. Allow ½″ on either side of the drawer for the glides. I affixed the drawer sides to the front with through joints, but while the finished product is lovely, the procedure is probably far too time-consuming for a desk that will be sold; if you use this joint, be sure to arrange the end grain so that it shows through (Illus. 14-12).

The inside of the drawer needn't be any deeper than two rows of diskettes, but the sides of the drawer should be longer so that full extension can be managed.

Illus. 14-10. This top view of the drawer shows how the sides of the drawer are longer than the drawer is deep to permit full extension without having to buy full-extension drawer glides. Be sure to leave ½″ on each side of the drawer glides.

To attach the drawer to the desk, screw through to the frame with 2″ x #10 flathead wood screws on one side, dado a piece into the other side, and screw that piece through to the top with 1¼″ x #10 flathead screws.

The next subassembly is the keyboard tray. While this was not a part of my original desk, it is probably the feature that contributes the most to its usefulness; by lowering the keyboard to just above lap height, I discovered that my net typing speed doubled in a very short period of time. The frame for this keyboard tray is tapered towards the front so that the typist won't at any time feel as though he or she is reaching in for the keys. The drawings don't show clearly that the sides and front are tapered to permit easy access to the keys. Dovetail the front and back onto the sides after cutting dadoes for the back of the actual keyboard tray; again, the excess length allows for full extension of the tray (Illus. 14-13–14-15). A certain amount of shaping should be done to the sides and front of this unit so that the keyboard sits slightly higher than any of the wooden parts.

If you are uncertain whether the bridge is for you, this is a good point at which to sand the unit to 220 grits and apply a finish of oil or varnish; I used three coats of Watco® Oil, scrubbing with

Illus. 14-11. New, smaller 3½″ diskettes adapted to the drawer.

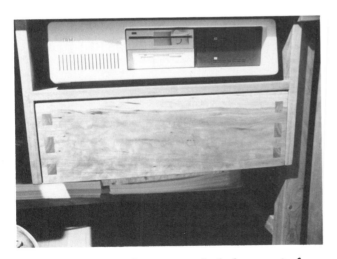

Illus. 14-12. Strive for symmetrical placement of end grain in the through joints on the drawer. If you are going to take the time to make this joint, make it as attractive as possible.

Illus. 14-13. This view of the keyboard tray shows the open space which provides the balance and full extension.

Illus. 14-14. This view of the keyboard tray shows it during normal use.

Illus. 14-15. This view of the underside of the keyboard tray shows that the hardware is mounted through a thin block to ensure that the keyboard passes freely under the apron.

600-grit abrasive after each coat. The unit is now ready for use.

The bridge is optional, but it is almost required if you are using two monitors because together they take up too much desk space. Now, even if I did not have the second monitor, I would want the bridge, for it brings the screen closer to eye level. My bridge is a piece of ⅝″ x 15″ x 40″ long hardwood that is fastened with screws into rabbets in a pair of 2 x 7s and then trimmed. The height of this bridge is just right for standing boxed diskettes under it, for holding all three of the IBM manuals in a stack, or, as now, for just housing a collection of material. That completes the unit for now; I'm sure that any additions to the equipment will add to the list of this desk's features.

In conclusion, there are a variety of considerations that should precede your building the computer desk. Some changes or variations might make your work infinitely more pleasant. First, all measurements should be subject to your (clients') needs: Consider your size, your room's size, and your computer's size. Alter any dimensions to suit these requirements.

Second, you must leave an opening for access to the computer's power switch, which all manufacturers seem to put on the back. Alternatively, you could use an external power unit such as the one you see in some of the illustrations; I recommend this approach because of the protection it provides against "glitches" in the electrical supply and because of the very high prices of replacing any part of a computer.

Illus. 14-16. This "work hole" in the top of the desk proved to be far more work than it was worth. Omitting it from your desk is definitely recommended.

Third, it would be useful to have access to the machine without having to pull the desk out from the wall. I built a hole into the top of my desk in hopes that it would give me access to the back panel for any changes I wanted to make (Illus. 14-16). This detail was not worth the effort; a more effective option would be moving the apron to the stand and having the top hinged, so one would have easier access to the internal workings of the computer. I regard the absence of this feature as the greatest single failing of my desk. Fourth, a shelf like the one in Illus. 14-8 and 14-9 is useful, especially if you are working in a small area like mine.

15.
Nightstand

To me, a bedside table should be the right height—that is, the *same* height as the bed, give or take no more than about 1½″. Thus, in modern bedrooms the stand should be about 19½″ high. Be sure to measure this against the beds in the area in which the nightstand will be featured. Because bedrooms seem to be chronically short of storage space, try to use a carcass design rather than a leg and apron design. This piece also presents you with an opportunity to try cutting dovetails. Some woodworkers will use a router and a dovetailing jig for this. Others will try cutting them by hand, following the instructions in Chapter 8. Try it by hand! A bit of practice will convince you that cutting dovetails by hand is recreational woodworking at its finest.

To build the project shown in Illus. 15-1 and 15-2, joint, plane, and glue up a panel around seven feet long. From it, crosscut the pieces which comprise the carcass. Next, cut out the base pieces, but save the drawer pieces "in the board" until later in the project.

Next, lay out the dovetails; it may be worth noting that the pins and tails are uniformly 1″ across the top, with the exception of the center one which is just over ¼″. You can vary this arrangement to suit your own taste without harming the strength or appearance of the project. Cut the base's dovetails, first sawing and then chiseling out the dovetails. Then, fit the four pieces together and plane them flat enough to use.

Next, start dovetailing the top. You may elect

Illus. 15-1. Nightstand. See the drawing on page 106.

to forego the dovetails at the bottom of the carcass, substituting there a reasonably handsome and quite serviceable joint created by cutting a very wide rabbet from the bottom of both side pieces, and then screwing the bottom into it at about 2″ intervals. By planning for this joint a little bit, you will be able to complete the joint without leaving the crude appearance of a rabbet joint: It is simply a question of accurately notching the bottom and leaving a "tab" on the sides.

Next, fasten the carcass to the base with wood screws and proceed to mount the framework that

Parts List for the Nightstand

Labels	Part	Material	Quantity	Thickness	Width	Length
A	Top	Hardwood	1	³/₄″	14½″	24″
B	Sides	Hardwood	2	³/₄″	14½″	15″
C	Bottom	Hardwood	1	³/₄″	14½″	23¼″
D	Base Side	Hardwood	2	³/₄″	3⅝″	12″
E	Base Front/ Rear	Hardwood	2	³/₄″	3⅝″	22″
F	Drawer Front	Hardwood	1	³/₄″	3″	22½″
G	Back	Plywood	1	¼″	14⅛″	23⅛″
	Drawer Side	Hardwood	2	³/₄″	2″	14″
	Drawer Rear	Hardwood	1	³/₄″	2″	22″
	Drawer Bottom	Masonite®	1	⅛″	12″	22″
	Drawer Support Side	Hardwood	2	³/₄″	2″	13¾″
	Drawer Support Front	Hardwood	1	³/₄″	2″	23½″
	Foot	Plastic or Metal Guides	4			

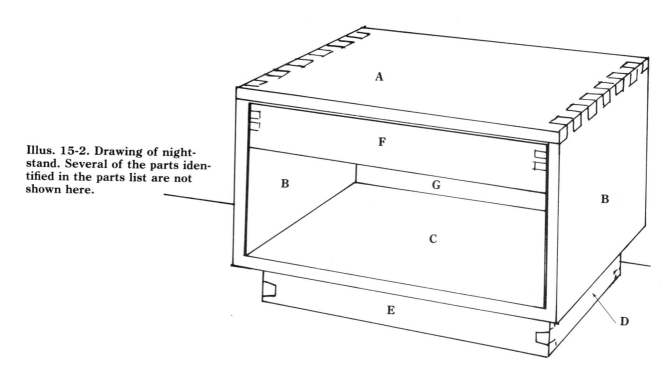

Illus. 15-2. Drawing of nightstand. Several of the parts identified in the parts list are not
shown here.

supports the small drawer. The drawer's purpose
is as much decorative as anything. The sides are
made of the same hardwood as is the front, and
they are through-dovetailed into the front, for this
makes a very strong joint. In a drawer this small,
there isn't a much faster way to join the front and
sides. The back of the drawer could also be dovetailed, but if you're willing to sacrifice a little bit
of drawer space to speed the process, you can cut
a pair of dadoes 1½″ from the back of the drawer's
side pieces. A pair of rabbets on the bottoms of
the drawer sides, and a corresponding saw kerf in
the front make mounting the drawer bottom with
glue and brads possible.

The frame on which the drawer rests can now
be put into place. Use the top of the carcass as
the guide to rout a ¾″ slot that is about ⅜″ deep.
Make several passes rather than one single pass
with the router. Slide the front frame in first, and
then attach the side pieces to it with splines while
you are gluing the side pieces in place. Cutting
out a hand-wide slot at the front center of the
drawer rest makes it possible to open the drawer
without having to mount a knob or pull on the

drawer, a feature you're sure to find most attractive (Illus. 15-3).

At this point, rout a rabbet in the back of the
carcass and square the corners with a chisel. Into
the rabbet mount a piece of ¼″ birch plywood. All
that remains is to sand the unit for finishing. After
the unit has been sanded well enough, begin the
process of applying a finish. The sturdiness of the
oil finish on the piece shown in this chapter became

Illus. 15-3. Note the cutout in the framework under
the drawer that permits the drawer to be opened
and closed without a handle.

apparent to me only lately, for this project was built about seven years ago and it has been moved about and seen more severe use than have many of my other projects, but it still looks fine.

The nightstand illustrated in this chapter was built years ago by my daughter (under my guidance), who was twelve years old at the time. If a twelve-year-old can build a piece this fine-looking, there is little excuse for your projects or mine not looking as good. Be willing to take your time, and don't be afraid to ask the advice of a more-experienced woodworker. The time will come when others will be coming to you for that advice.

16.
Folding Nightstand

You may wish to alter the sizes of some of these pieces to more closely meet the requirements of the intended setting for your table. Not much material is used for this table (Illus. 16-1–16-4), so you should be willing to use top-quality material.

The first step in building the table is cutting all the pieces to size. A good first step in doing this is to glue up the boards that will form your top; your goal is a 24″-diameter circle, so pieces very slightly longer than that should be glued to form a panel very slightly wider than that. If you biscuit-join the pieces together as an alignment aid, you may want to draw the circle on the pieces before you do the actual joining (Illus. 16-5–16-7); having a biscuit show through an edge would be very disappointing, to say the least.

We set the table saw's mitre gauge to 3° off-square to get the taper in the legs and other pieces. This means that the apron pieces can be cut one after another if you flip the board so that both ends taper out. The tops and bottoms of the legs must be cut to the same 3° off-square, so they line up. Fit the cross-braces by eye before cutting the 3° tapers on them; they will slide directly into place. Even the tops and bottoms of the legs should be tapered so the top can sit flat.

Lay out the curves for the aprons with an adjustable curve (Illus. 16-8). Then cut them out with a band saw or with a hand-held sabre saw. After cutting, sand them with a drum sander mounted in your drill press. After these pieces are

ready, attach them to the legs. We used two #20 biscuits at each leg, and then clamped the pieces together, clamping at both the top and bottom of the leg sets.

Now the cross-brace can be fitted in. We attached these braces by cross-drilling (also known as angle-drilling) for dowels. The dowel enters the

Illus. 16-1. The folding nightstand.

Parts List for the Folding Nightstand

Label	Part	Quantity	Thickness	Width	Length
A	Top	1	$\frac{3}{4}''$	24″ Diameter	
B	Apron	3	$\frac{3}{4}''$	8″	$14\frac{1}{2}''$
C	Leg	6	$\frac{3}{4}''$	$1\frac{7}{8}''$	$27\frac{1}{2}''$
D	Cross-Brace*	3	$\frac{3}{4}''$	$1\frac{3}{4}''$	$16\frac{1}{2}''$
	Hinges	4			
	Dowels**	3	$\frac{3}{8}''$	1″ in diameter	

*The size of the brace is variable, depending upon where you wish to position it.
  We recommend that you check this by eye before cutting your stock.
**The dowels are used to position the top on the leg set.

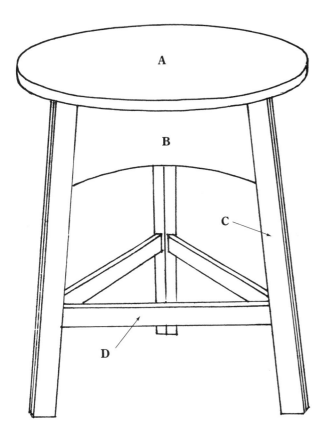

Illus. 16-2. A drawing of the folding nightstand.

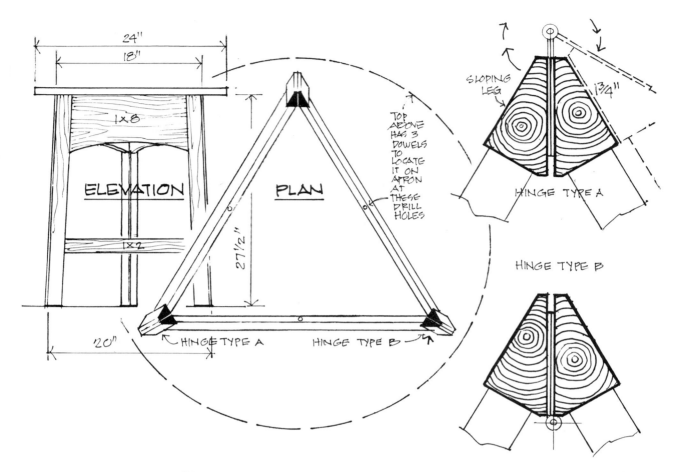

Illus. 16-3. The elevation and plan for the nightstand, and drawings of the hinges used in it.

cross-brace from the bottom, and then enters the leg at an angle. While doing this, we learned that cutting the 30° angle on the "inside" of each leg did *not* cut the dowels, so if we were to do it again, we might prefer to use pocket holes and screws (Illus. 16-9).

After each of the three leg units is complete, saw them at 30° (Illus. 16-10) and mount your hinges. We used Lamello Paumelle Hinges (Illus. 16-11) for several reasons: They are very attractive, we had them in the shop, and, perhaps most importantly, because they slip-fit they permit the three pieces of the total leg set to be taken apart at will. Illus. 16-3 shows how these hinges work. They are made for mounting in biscuit slots, but

if you're using a joiner that is not very versatile, you may prefer to just surface-mount them. The hinges are available in black, nickel plate, or solid brass; use the color that you like best. Despite all these arguments in favor of the Lamello hinges, it's perfectly okay to substitute other hinges.

Drill the top center of each leg set for a ³⁄₈″ dowel; a ¹⁄₂″-deep hole should suffice. Set a dowel center into each hole and carefully position the base on the underside of the table. A couple of taps will mark the drilling locations on the underside of the top.

After this step has been completed, all that remains is to sand the pieces and apply your favorite finish.

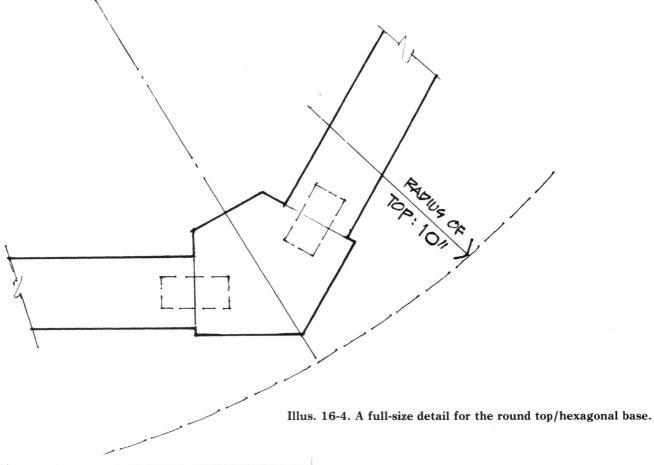

Illus. 16-4. A full-size detail for the round top/hexagonal base.

RADIUS OF TOP: 10"

Illus. 16-5. Here is a handy circle layout tool. In a fairly long piece of 1 x 2, drill a series of pencil-size holes 1″ apart. At one end, space a series of nail-size holes for fractions. Use a punch to mark the spot the nail will ride in as the pencil goes around it. Be sure the punch mark goes on the bottom of the surface, and is no more than hand-pressure deep.

Illus. 16-6. The pieces glued up
so the circle can be cut.

Illus. 16-7. We used two sizes of router bits to finish the tabletop's edge, a larger bit on the underside of the top and a smaller one on the upper surface. We set each so that they left approximately
$\frac{1}{32}$″ of off-set at the top. Then we used the random
orbit sander to bring the edges down to flush.

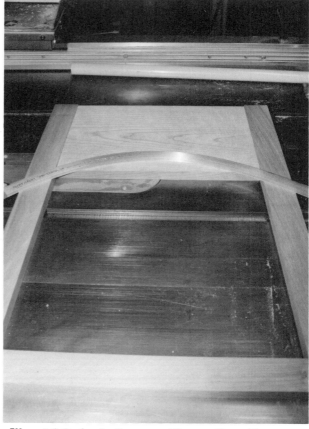

Illus. 16-8. Apply the arc with an adjustable curve.

Illus. 16-9. A radial arm drill press like this is useful for drilling the pocket holes for attaching the lower cross-braces.

Illus. 16-10. Be sure to use a featherboard to help hold the work in place when you saw the 30° angles on each side of the leg sets.

Illus. 16-11 (left). Lamello Paumelle Hinges feature left- and right-hand openings. Apply them to the leg sets so the pin is always facing "up," to ensure that the table stays together better if you have to pick it up to move it.

17.
Butcher Block Table

You've seen butcher block tables in stores and catalogues. They invariably seem too light, too cheaply made, or far too expensive. After we decided we wanted one, I looked at every commercial model I could find, and used what I learned to make the butcher block table shown here (Illus. 17-1–17-10). You can build this in an ordinarily equipped shop with finest grade materials for around $100.

I start each project with rough lumber and usually figure how much will be used by multiplying the square footage of the finished product by a waste factor of 1.30; this covers end-of-rough-stock loss, matching, and occasional mistakes, and there is still enough material left over for a "shorts" rack. If you use the same formula, you can build this project with just 20 board feet of 2″ maple and 30 board feet of 1″ maple. Since the wood will cost only around $60, you should be able to afford the top-quality casters recommended later in the chapter.

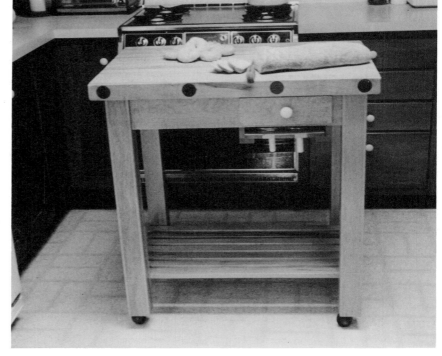

Illus. 17-1. Butcher block table. Also see Illus. 7-2–7-10 and page G of the color section.

Parts List for the Butcher Block Table

Label	Part*	Quantity	Thickness	Width	Length
A	Leg Piece	8	¾″	3″	31″
B	Leg Piece	8	¾″	2½″	31″
C	Top	1	2½″	24″	36″
D	Short Apron	2	¾″	4½″	16″
E	Long Apron	2	¾″	4½″	26½″
F	Slat Shelf Support	2	¾″	2¼″	20½″
G	Slats	7	¾″	1¾″	31″
H	Leg End Caps	8	¾″	2½″	2½″
I	Drawer Hangers	3	¾″	4″	21″**
J	Drawer Hangers for Processor Option	2	¾″	7″	21″
K	Side Rails for Outsides	2	½″	1″	21″
L	Side Rails for Insides	2	½″	¾″	21″
M	Optional Rail Ends	2	¾″	2″	12″
N	Optional Rails	3	¾″	2″	17″
O	Top Hold-Downs	2	¾″	2″	15″
P	Top Hold-Downs	2	¾″	2″	25½″

Continue on Following Page

Label	Part*	Quantity	Thickness	Width	Length
Q	Drawer Sides	4	³⁄₄″	22″	21″
R	Drawer Front	2	³⁄₄″	3″	13″
S	Drawer Back	2	³⁄₄″	1⁷⁄₈″	11½″
T	Masonite® Drawer Bottoms	2	⅛″	11½″	21″

*All pieces are made of maple unless otherwise noted.
**All pieces labelled 21″ long must be trimmed to fit.

Supplies

1 six-foot-long threaded rod
6 nuts with washers for rod
Four 2¼″ Shepherd® casters and plate mount
2 pulls to match your room's decor
Adhesive

Abrasive
Martens™ Wood Preservative
Behlen® Salad Bowl Finish
½″ dowel for locking joints
1½″ x #8 flathead brass screws

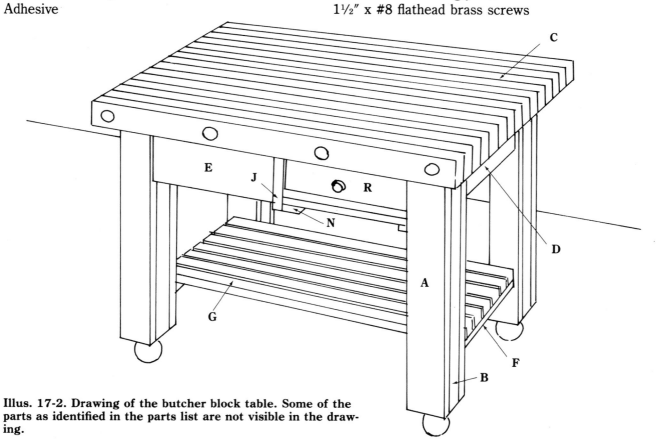

Illus. 17-2. Drawing of the butcher block table. Some of the parts as identified in the parts list are not visible in the drawing.

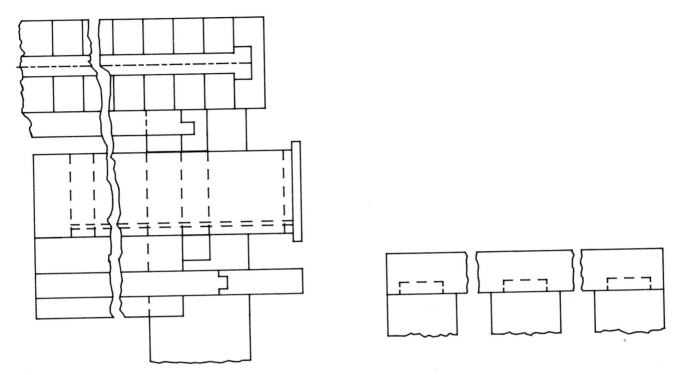

Illus. 17-3. Above left: A side view of the apron showing the drawer and tray for food processor accessories. Above right: End view of the joints at either end of the tray.

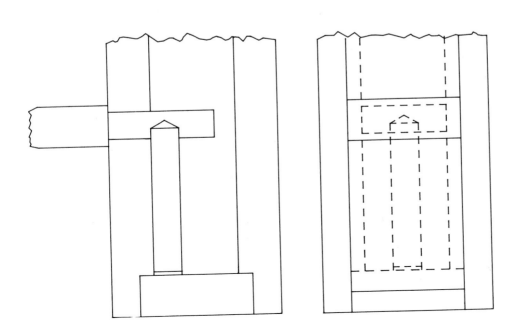

Illus. 17-4. Two views of the joinery that attaches the low shelf.

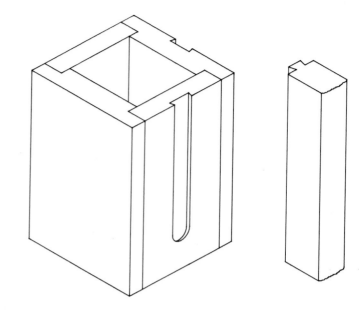

Illus. 17-5. How the legs are assembled. Dovetail joinery holds the apron pieces in place.

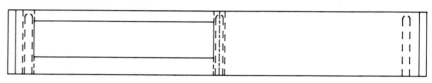

Illus. 17-6. A view of the apron from either face; one drawer opens to each face.

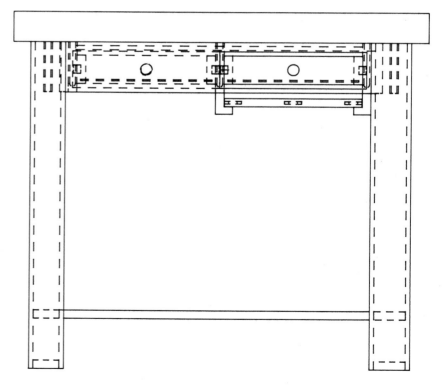

Illus. 17-7. An overall front view.

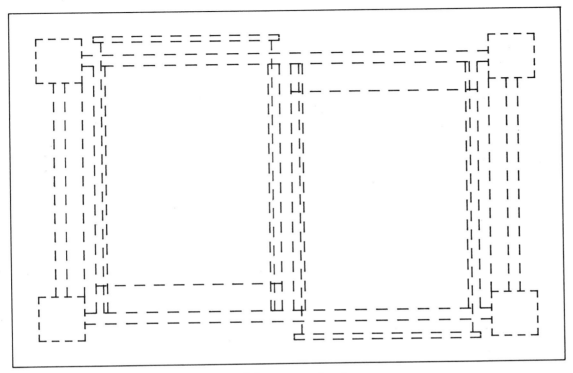

Illus. 17-8. A top view of the aprons and drawer mechanisms.

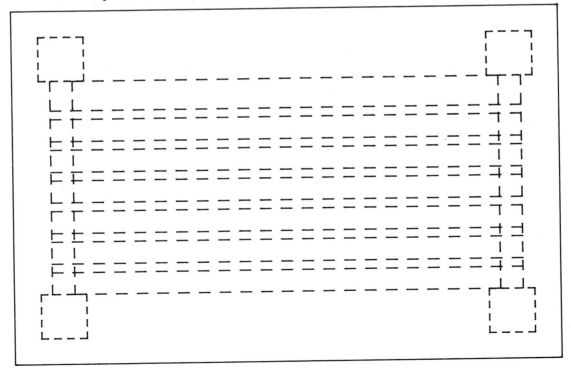

Illus. 17-9. A view of the table from the bottom.

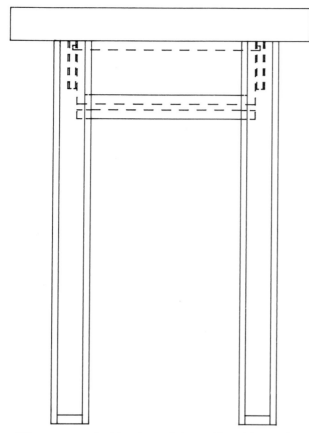

Illus. 17-10. A side view of the table without the drawers.

I built the first of these tables for myself more than a decade ago. I have replenished the oil on the top occasionally. It looks better now than it ever did, and I am still on my first bottle of preservative. Here is my best measure of its strength: At least once a month since it was new, I have made eight dozen bagels on it—that's heavy kneading by hand. Indeed, I built it specifically for that task, so in my kitchen it is called a bagel block table.

Let's begin with some design considerations. My bagel block table is just short of 2' wide by 3' long; it might have been longer and wider, but I was building at the time with an impoverished stock of at-hand materials and an empty billfold. Further, if the table is more than 2', you may run into problems fine-planing the top. Actually, an

even slightly smaller unit would do most American kitchens nicely.

The positioning of the shelf could be a bit higher; in a smaller kitchen, the microwave oven could be placed on this shelf, and one certainly wouldn't want to operate that appliance from one's knees! The work surface is 35″ from the floor—that's a perfect height for me, at 5'11", to knead big batches of bakery. Be sure to adjust the height to your user and task.

Whether you are redesigning or using my plan, fabricate the top first. Cut pieces of mixed thickness to 24″ wide x 36″ long. Make a jig so that you can easily drill the matching $7/16$ hole (assuming you are using $3/8$″ threaded rod for your internal clamping) at the center of the board and on the centerline about 4″ from either end. This jig is no more than a board with some stops clamped to it that is clamped to your drill press. Glue up using the threaded rod as clamps through the holes you have already drilled; the threaded rod will be left in place as a permanent part of the top. Of course, you will want to use clamps, too. I used resorcinol cement on my first butcher-block top, but I have come to understand that that was a basically needless expense.

There are two ways to cover the threaded rods that clamp the piece together. The first way is to drill holes that match your largest plug cutter, and cover the nuts with plugs. An alternative is to drill the holes on the inside of the outside pieces, and glue on the two outside strips last. I find this latter method more attractive.

Make this top well. It uses nearly 20 board feet of material, so is the most expensive single piece in the project; it is also the most used and visible part of the project.

After you have scraped off the excess glue, have your top planed in a powerful, sharp industrial planer. Someone in a local industry will rent you time on a machine this large; if you are lucky, you may be able to rent time on something like a 36″ two-sided abrasive planer.

After the top has been planed to your satisfaction, sand it dead flat. Use a round-over router bit to round all corners and edges. Finish-sand through 220 grit and apply your finish. There are two suitable finishes which are absolutely non-toxic: Behlen® Salad Bowl Finish and Martens™ Wood Preservative. I use Behlen® Salad Bowl Finish for the first coat, and then I put one application of Marten's on all surfaces of the top daily until it is mounted on the base.

The first step in making the base is fabricating the legs. Because their dimensions are 3″ x 3″ x 31″, they would be too heavy and you'd probably have to glue up to get 3 x 3 material anyway, so for each leg cut 4 pieces, two ¾″ x 3″ x 31″ and two ¾″x 2½″ x 31″. With a saw or router cut a rabbet ¾″ wide x ½″ deep from all four edges of the 3″-wide piece; do likewise to just the ends of the 2½″-wide piece. Glue up the hollow legs with 2½″-square caps at the top and bottom, but don't glue in the caps yet. By the time you have rounded over all edges, you'll realize that you have face grain now facing in all directions, giving the legs a very handsome appearance.

After you have scraped the glue from the legs and planed and sanded them absolutely smooth, use a dovetail router bit to cut a dovetail channel for the apron pieces; the channel should be 4″ long x ½″ wide; there should be two cuts per leg, eight altogether. Whether these channels should be centered or placed nearer the outside edges of the legs is a debatable point. That they need to oppose one another directly is not debatable.

Next, make the apron pieces. You need two ¾″ x 4½″ x 16″ and two ¾″ x 4½″ x 26½″ pieces. Dovetail the ends of these to fit the channels in the legs. Then lay the two long pieces together with their "top" edges touching. Scribe a center-line across them; then mark ⅜″ on either side of that centerline; these new lines represent the out-side edges of the center board that will hold your drawers. From these lines measure over 12″.

Now, scribe lines horizontally on each piece so that you have 2⅛″ x 12″ holes marked. Cut out these holes by using stop cuts on a table saw and finishing with a handsaw, using a router and a chisel or using a jigsaw if you have one. Rout a

⅜″ dado ⅜″ from the top inside each apron piece; this dado will hold the 2″ piece through which the top is screwed to the base. Cut a corresponding ¾″ x 2″ piece with an appropriate tongue for the dadoes just made in the apron pieces.

The next step on these apron pieces is to cut cross slots for drawer hanger units. This time, lay the pieces out so their inside bottoms come to-gether. Mark ½″ from the top right alongside each drawer opening. With a router and a T-square cut dovetail slots to the mark at each of your three marked spots. Now, finally, you can fit these apron pieces to the legs.

With the aprons dry-mounted, mount the slat tray near the bottom of the unit (Illus. 17-11). Mark 4″ from the bottom. With a ⅝″ straight bit, cut 1½″ horizontal channels that face one another across the short apron ends. Cut two pieces 2¼″ wide x 20½″ long. Cut a ⅝″ x 1½″ x 2¼″ long tenon on each end of each piece. Dry-fit these pieces to the unit. This, of course, involves taking the appropriate apron rails out first.

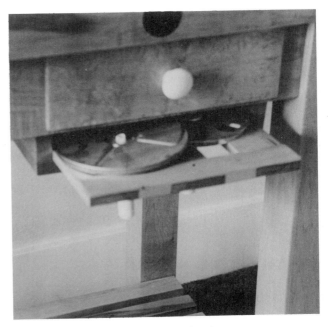

Illus. 17-11. A close-up of the food processor acces-sory tray.

When you are satisfied with the fit, mark inside the legs for a locking joint. The joint on my table is just a ½″ hole that doesn't extend quite all the way through; I drove a flattened dowel through that hole. The dowel is long enough to reach but not quite touch the cap, so there is no danger of its falling out. When you are satisfied with the fit, glue the base unit together. The locking joint on the bottom crosspiece doesn't have to be glued.

Affix 7 pieces, ¾″ x 1¾″ x 31″, to the bottom crosspieces; these are your slat shelf members. Use countersunk 1¼″ x #8 flathead wood screws to fasten them flush to outside edges, and space the remainder by the thickness of a single board; thus, the centerpiece may be slightly narrower or wider than the others.

While you have the 1¼″ x #8 screws handy, screw the top and bottom caps into the legs. Completing the drawer mechanisms is the next step. Measure across the dovetails cut in the aprons, and cut 3 pieces 4″ wide by about 21″ long. The length depends upon your placement of the apron on the legs and upon the depth of your dovetail slot. Be sure to measure twice, so you will only have to cut once. Cut a dovetail on the end of each piece, and test-fit each piece. Then, cut ½″ wide x ½″ deep dadoes lengthwise in the middle of each opposing piece. Don't dado through the middle piece; those pieces can be each only ½″ deep. Fit a ½″ x 1″ piece into each dado, and a ½″ x ¾″ piece in either side of the middle since you reduced the depth of those dadoes. Glue these pieces neatly in place.

An option some cooks might appreciate would be to substitute 6½ ″ or 7″ material on one side for the drawer hanger. As Illus. 17-1 shows, this provides better storage for food processor tools than you have seen commercially. All it involves is a bracket on each end, and a mortised-and-tenoned rack to hold your food processor cutters. To make this rack, you need 2 pieces ¾″ x 2″ x 12″ and 3 pieces ¾″ x 2″ x 17″; this last dimension should be checked for the same reason the 21″ dimension was checked on the drawer hangers. Cut your mortise-and-tenon joints, and when ev-

erything fits to your satisfaction, glue the rack together neatly.

Now that your base is ready to accept drawers, it is time to make drawers. You need two pieces ¾″ x 2″ x a length equal to the back of the cavity (and like the aforementioned 17″ and 21″ dimensions, this one must be measured during construction). Cut dadoes or rabbets for the ⅛″ Masonite® bottom, and dadoes for the drawer glides; these dadoes should be carefully fitted before cutting. The dadoes for the drawer backs require less thought; just put them opposite one another far enough from the back that the drawer won't fall out when its contents are fully visible.

After these cuts are made, the 1⅞″ x 11½″ back will be ready to be glued in place, as will the Masonite drawer bottom. The only piece left to fabricate for the drawer is the front. From a 3″ wide x 13″ long blank, cut a rabbet ½″ deep x ½″ wide on the top, one that is ⅝″ wide on the bottom and one 1¼″ wide on each side. After sanding the pieces, assemble the drawer with glue and tacks and mount a knob or pull of your choice (Illus. 17-12). If hardware to match the kitchen is unavailable, plain white porcelain knobs or shop-made wooden pulls would be my first choices.

After you have final-fit the drawers, it is time

Illus. 17-12. A close-up of the drawer detail.

to finish the base unit. My units got applications of Watco® Natural Danish Oil, followed by a buffing with Gillespie's Lemon Oil. Watco Oil seems to me to be the best of the oil finishes, but any lemon oil (more properly lemongrass oil) will do. Buy a big can: A gallon costs about as much as four pints, and it lasts forever.

An alternative to this finishing schedule would be to finish it to match the kitchen; at the risk of pricing the table out of your price range, it would be possible to use even the same material as your kitchen for the base rather than the maple. Maple is not essential to the project, but I cannot imagine making the top of anything else.

Mount the Shepherd #9213 casters; Shepherd casters cost more than other casters, but are of top-quality construction, are suitable for a hard or carpeted floor, have a lifetime guarantee, and are able to withstand weight and abuse they are sure to get on a unit like this. Mount the top with half a dozen large screws, say 1½" or 2" by #10. Use screws that are around the shop rather than buying special ones.

Give the top another coat of Martens Wood Preservative, and then deliver the unit with whatever's left over in the bottle of preservative. After all, using the whole bottle in this way makes figuring the cost of finishing materials easier.

If you have a market for several such tables, you would save a great deal of time and money by making them at once.

Amazingly, the butcher block table is one kitchen appliance that is a real energy saver: I can't imagine my kitchen without one. In fact, if I had to I'd keep my butcher block instead of the kitchen table at which we eat.

18.
Simple Kitchen Table

Though it's as good looking as anything on the market, this graceful kitchen table (Illus. 18-1–18-3) can be built and perhaps finished in a single weekend. The key to building this table so quickly is the use of biscuit joints. Of course, the dimensions of the parts in the cutting list may be altered for different needs or different types of tables.

After you have acquired suitable stock, joint and plane it to the proper dimensions. You're far more likely to get full 2 x 2 legs from 2″ stock if you cut it slightly oversize while the lumber is still rough, and then joint and plane minimally to make

legs from single pieces. This is far more attractive than gluing legs from two or more pieces of 1″ stock. You can shape the corners of the legs, aprons, etc. either before or after slotting for your biscuits. The important part is that the stock be as ready to finish as possible before gluing.

Sort the pieces for the top, and then joint their edges until they are flat and square enough to be glued. After joining them, make one pass with an edge-trimming block plane on each edge to be glued in order to "spring" the joints, so they'll be less likely to break as the wood dries with the

Illus. 18-1. Simple kitchen table. Also see page H of the color section.

passage of time. Arrange the pieces for the most attractive panel, and mark the arrangement.

Glue up the stock for the tops. Biscuit joining is one of the easiest ways to align the stock for the top. Cut slots for biscuits 2″–3″ from the ends and at 6–10″ intervals between them. I still prefer to glue and clamp only two pieces at a time, although this is not necessary when using biscuit joints. This means gluing pieces A-B, C-D, and E-F as shown in Illus. 18-2 and 18-3 and clamping each pair separately. Then glue pieces AB-CD or CD-EF. Then glue the remaining two pieces. Another way of ensuring a flat top is gluing the top in a veneer press or with the Plano clamping system.

Whichever method you use, after each gluing remove any excess glue when it hardens to about the consistency of cottage cheese. Accuracy in stock preparation and biscuit joinery should pro-

Parts List for the Simple Kitchen Table

Label	Part	Quantity	Thickness	Width	Length
A	Leg	4	2″	2″	28¼″–29¼″
B	Top	1	⅞″	32″	36″
C	Apron	2	⅞″	3″	24″
D	Apron	2	⅞″	3″	28″
E	Brace	2	⅞″	2″	24″
F	Brace	2	⅞″	2″	28″

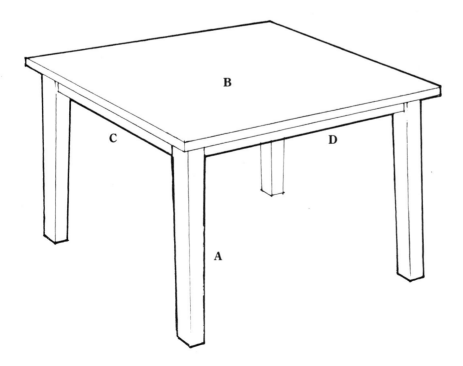

Illus. 18-2. Drawing of simple kitchen table. Also see Illus. 18-3.

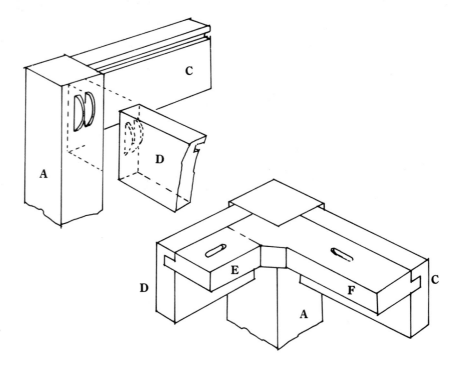

Illus. 18-3. The wooden assembly for attaching the top to the apron.

duce a panel flat enough that you can clean it up with light planing, scraping, and/or a pad sander.

Prepare your apron pieces by biscuiting the 2" x 24" brace pieces to the 3" x 24" aprons, and the 2" x 28" braces to the 3" x 28" aprons. A second way of doing this would be to use table irons and a narrower kerf. Alternatively, the apron could be dadoed about 3/8" from the tops and about 1/2" deep, and the brace could be rabbeted to "float" in these slots, thereby permitting the top to be tightly fastened to the braces.

Attach the apron pieces to the leg pieces with double biscuits. Mark the joints 1½" from the "inside" top sides of each leg and at the middle of the end of each apron piece. Use a spacer block either 1/8" or 1/4" thick when cutting the slots on the apron pieces, so that the apron will be slightly inseted from the legs.

Cutting the second row of biscuit slots will require resetting the biscuit joiner and going all around the legs and apron pieces again unless you have a second spacer block handy for use on all the cuts the second time around. I find using a

pair of spacer blocks to be the quicker and more accurate method.

Cut slots all the way around the leg assembly. Since you will be making two cuts per surface, and there are two surfaces per joint, and four joints per leg, and 4 legs, this equals a total of 32 slots for 16 biscuits (2 x 2 x 4 x 4 = 64 cuts ÷ 2, for 32 slots for 16 biscuits).

Glue the slots and the end grain; end grain glued to long grain won't hold, but the glue does seal the end grain from moisture. Assemble the apron pieces to the legs with #20 biscuits. I have found this works best if I assemble first two pairs of legs, and then join them with the matching cross apron pieces.

Finish shaping the top, legs, and apron assemblies before doing the final assembly. I went around the top with a 1/4" round-over bit on both the upper and under surfaces. You may have a different decoration in mind. All but final sanding of the top should be done before assembly. I used the same 1/4" round-over bit on both the inside and outside surfaces of the apron bottoms and on all four corners of each leg. For these loose pieces, I found it easier, quicker, and safer to push the wood through a setup on my router table than it would have been to bring the router to the work.

If you want to cut ½″ of taper into the insides of the legs, do this before using the round-over bit.

It's probably not absolutely necessary, but I prefer to do my biscuit joining while the pieces are still absolutely square. After I test-fit the square pieces, I start the routing and sanding that will lead me to the more curvaceous finished product.

After the leg set's glue has dried, and you have finish-sanded the unit, set the top top-down on a pair of sawhorses or a padded workbench. Center the leg set, and attach it using whichever method you have selected from the choices outlined above. Four screws should be sufficient to hold the top in place; drill the pilot holes in the braces slightly oversize to allow for seasonal movement of the wood.

After the base has been screwed to the top, flip the assembly over, fine-sand the unit, wipe off all the fine dust, and finish with your choice of finishing products. Lately, I've been using Hydro-cote® satin polyurethane, which provides a superior finish in about three or four coats, all of which can be applied in the same afternoon. Indeed, this finish, which is best applied with a rag (and rubber gloves) or an inexpensive foam brush (which can be rinsed out in water and reused) is a key reason why the table can be completed in a weekend. After the fourth coat of polyurethane has dried, apply a coat of wax with a piece of #0 3M Scotch-Brite® pad and buff the wax to a fine sheen.

When even a simple project like this consumes a total of upwards of 50 biscuits, you can see how quickly packages of biscuits will disappear in your shop. This handsome project serves as a worthy introduction to biscuit joinery and is designed so it can be modified for other uses.

19.
Designer Kitchen Table

The customer who buys a piece of furniture from me is almost always buying a prototype. The client and I talk about the nature of design and the particular problem(s) that we are to solve with the project. The challenge in this instance was to build a solid-wood kitchen table big enough to seat six people in a very small kitchen. I suggested a simple round pedestal table, but when the size of the standard pedestal base became evident, that notion was quickly rejected. I recalled the tables of the type that decorated many living rooms in our younger, poorer days. These tables were made of a telephone cable spool. We had once cut one in half, and each half stood just fine.

I proposed a pedestal like that about 20″ in diameter under a 48″ top, and my client suggested

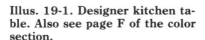

Illus. 19-1. Designer kitchen table. Also see page F of the color section.

128

Parts List for the Designer Kitchen Table

Label	Part	Quantity	Thickness	Width	Length
A	Hex Sides	12	1¾″	3″	10″
B	Plywood Hex Liner	6	½″	6½″	28″
C	Dowels	24 (36)	⅞″ Diameter	⅞″	26½″
D	Top	1	1¼″	48″ Diameter	
	Splines	12	½″	4½″	3″
	1½″ x #10 sheet-metal screws	24			
	1¼″ x #8 flathead screws	24			

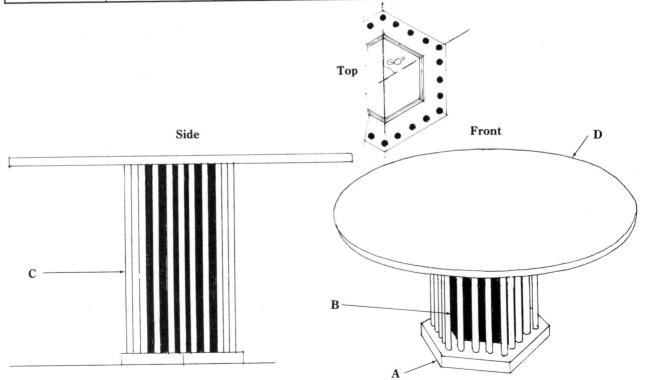

Illus. 19-2. A drawing showing the top, front, and side views of the designer kitchen table.

Illus. 19-3. A close-up of the base.

that the base be made of spindles rather than solid stock. I agreed that this might be possible, sketched it, and proceeded to build it (Illus. 19-1–19-3).

The top is solid maple, 1¼″ thick, 48″ in diameter. I glued up random-width pieces until I had two pieces 25″ x 50″, slightly shorter near the "outside" edges to prevent some waste at cut-out time. I took these pieces out for planing, jointed them to a precise fit, cut those jointed surfaces for a spline (using a ¼″ slotting bit in my router), glued them together, and left this large, flat piece in the clamps while I made the base.

Cutting the round top was a simple matter of setting up a circle-cutting router jig (which, in this case, consisted of a piece of Masonite screwed to both the router and the exact center of the table's bottom surface in such a way that the cutter was 24″ from the center) and walking around the table, taking between ⅛″ and ¼″ at a pass. After the waste was cut off the slab, a decorative cut with a ¾″ round-over bit completed the sides; the cut of this mighty bit was so clean that little edge-sanding was needed.

Some have suggested that the project would be even more attractive with a hexagonal top. I agree, but my client did not. In most ways, the round top is more practical.

Because we wanted something of a butcher-block effect, the top was fine-sanded, and the process of building up an oil finish was begun. After a couple of coats of Minwax® Walnut Oil had a chance to polymerize, we started to apply Martens Wood Preservative daily until delivery, leaving the balance of the bottle with the client. Make sure you use a finish like Martens Wood Preservative or Behlen Salad Bowl Finish on woodwork that may regularly encounter food. These finishes are nontoxic.

The base consists of two hexagons, each formed of six 1¾″ x 3″ x 10″ maple pieces joined at 60° at the ends with splines of contrasting wood. These splines are glued and screwed into place.

When you make these dozen pieces that form these hexagons, cut a 30° angle on each end of the 10″ boards, so the inside length of each is 6½″. If these boards are accurately cut, any six of them should form a perfect hexagon. Cut a ½″ wide x 1½″ deep slot full width across the newly angled ends. Glued and screwed splines of like or contrasting wood are the main means of holding the hexagons together; they come from a piece of stock 4¼″ wide x 3″ long; be sure to note that each of these spline pieces is wider than it is long. The grain must run the same direction as the hexagon; if you glue cross-grain, you are almost sure to experience some breakage in later steps. I cut each of my dozen splines on the band saw to a slight "wing" shape, so I would have less hand-shaping to do after gluing.

I didn't like the price of ⅞″ dowels, so I set out to make some. I cut a stack of ⅞″ x ⅞″ x 26½″ pieces, and gave each piece four passes over a 5⁄16″ round-over bit on a router table. That made them essentially, though not precisely, round. I mounted my ⅞″ plug cutter on my mortising table and rigged a quick-clamping jig that would ensure me 1″ of perfectly round tenon at each end of each piece. This operation went very fast.

I let the pieces sit a week while I went about some other business; the week's sitting made it much easier to pick out the two dozen straightest pieces, the pieces least chipped in the manufacturing process.

After the two hexagons are glued, dried, screwed, shaped, and sanded, drill holes in them for the dowels. I marked out the hexagons using a standard marking gauge, marked off each of the six sides into fourths, and drilled $7/8''$ holes at the three marked spots on each side. After these 18 holes were drilled in each piece, I drilled another six, each where the scribed line intersected with one of the hexagon's joints. It was easy to fit the $7/8''$ pieces into these holes.

For the second hexagon, you'll need help with lining up the dowels and the holes. Six or eight extra hands might be needed. With a mallet, drive the dowels home. Adhesive isn't necessary, but it might be a good idea to cross-dowel each end of at least one dowel per side. If you had sanded all the members quite thoroughly as you completed them, the base is ready for finishing. Apply the

finish to the top minus the Martens Wood Preservative. Attach the top to the base with two $1\frac{1}{2}''$ x $\frac{1}{4}''$ hex-headed lag bolts.

When I assembled the table with bolts in the client's kitchen, I observed that there was about $\frac{1}{2}''$ of lateral, almost spiralled torsion in the table, so I suggested to the client that she reject the project. She decided that it was too good-looking to reject, so we left it in place. All it took was a week to realize that the piece in its present form was unhandy and potentially dangerous. After puzzling over the alternatives for several days, we determined that I would find a sheet of nicely matching plywood and cut a full-length liner for each of the hexagons' six shared sides, producing another hexagon, this one on the side of the interiors of the other two, with nicely mitred sides. This piece was fastened to the main unit—after oiling, of course—with two $1\frac{1}{2}''$ x #10 sheet-metal screws at each end. This repair took only just over an hour, and the table is now absolutely rigid, and, amazingly enough, it is even better looking than it was before.

20.
Peter Mader's Harvest Table

Peter Mader's harvest table provides proof that one doesn't need a fully equipped workshop to do fine woodworking. This large, handsome table (Illus. 20-1–20-4) was made using commercial-grade planed timbers, a table saw, and a band saw.

Because Mader hasn't yet acquired a jointer, he has worked up a way of gluing large panels without jointing the individual boards (Illus. 20-5–20-8). First, he bought the straightest possible boards. For this table, Mader bought four 8' long 1 x 12s. Each of them was cut in half lengthwise with a standard "rip" blade; then he cleaned up the edges by setting the saw in about 1/16" and recutting them with a fine-toothed plywood blade.

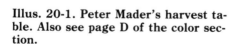
Illus. 20-1. Peter Mader's harvest table. Also see page D of the color section.

Alternating pieces were flipped end-over-end in order to alternate grain and help keep the material flat as it was glued up. Paying careful attention to detail is the key to success here. The material is ready to glue when the edges are straight or slightly concave. The plywood blade leaves just enough roughness on the edges of the board to enhance adhesion. This is a technique that might prove helpful in your shop, especially if you haven't the means or the space to add a jointer to your workshop.

The trestle legs were each made from a single commercial 2 x 8 that is 8′ long. First, the pieces were ripped to half-width. Then each piece was sawed to a thickness of 1″, and the pieces were reglued. Lacking sophisticated mortising equip-

Parts List for the Harvest Table

Label	Part	Quantity	Thickness	Width	Length
A	Top	1	1″	36″	93″
B	Cross Rail	1	1½″	4″	65″
C	Foot	2	2″	2¾″	30″
D	"Leg"	2	1″	13″	25¾″
E	Lock Piece	2	1½″*	1⅝″	4″
	Top Support	2	2″	3¾″	30″

*The lock piece tapers to 1″

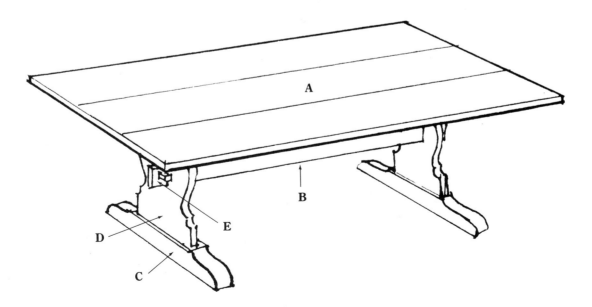

Illus. 20-2. Drawing of the harvest table.

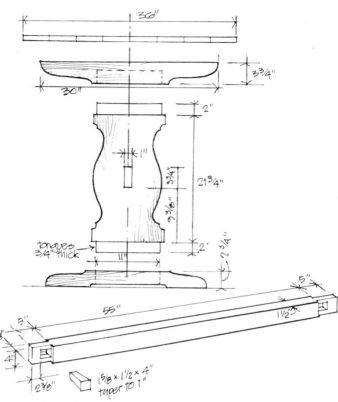

Illus. 20-3 (above left). End view of the table. Illus. 20-4 (above right). This end-view sketch reveals everything you need to know in order to build the table.

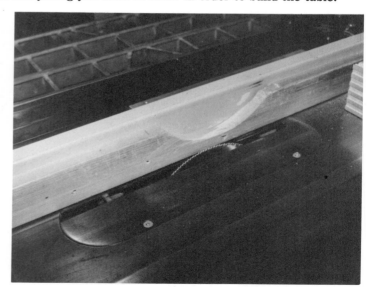

Illus. 20-5 (above left). Peter Mader demonstrating the cut that eliminates the need to joint the stock. Illus. 20-6 (above right). A close-up of the blade and spacer that help to ensure straight work.

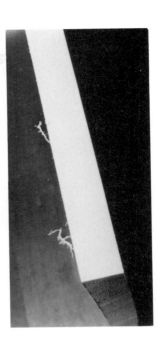

Illus. 20-7 (above left). This close-up shows how little stock is removed with the fine-tooth plywood-cutting blade. Illus. 20-8
(above right). This little bit of fuzz indicates the kind of surface
that helps to make this joint so successful.

Illus. 20-9. The through tenon that holds the leg
set together.

ment, Mader cut *half* of each mortise on each side
before gluing the center together (Illus. 20-9).
Another advantage of this method is that it allows
you to stack the pieces for cutting the curves in
the band saw; someone who has no band saw could
use a scroll saw or even a coping saw (sometimes
called a fretsaw) with equal effect. The top and
bottom pieces of the trestle, those that actually
meet the floor, and the table surface are glued up
to 2″ thick after half-mortises are cut from either
side (Illus. 20-10 and 20-11).

After the three parts of each end unit have been
glued, the stretcher is made from a piece of 2 x
4 that is 6′ long. After a 6″ piece has been cut
from one end to use for the locking pins, the piece
is ripped in half, half-mortise holes are cut in place
on the table saw, and the piece is glued back together. Then 5″ of material is removed from the
sides of either end of the stretcher, so that the
piece looks like the piece in Illus. 20-4. The
stretcher can be wedged in place at this time if
you wish to use the base as a support for any of
the steps in gluing the top.

The top was glued up from 7 strips cut from
four 1 x 12s that are 8′ long, each of which had

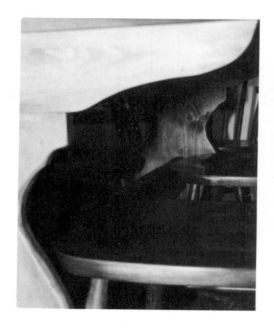

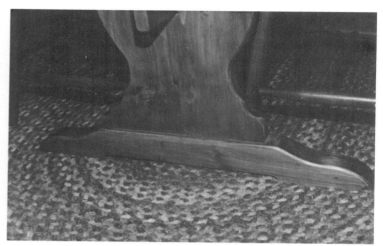

Illus. 20-10 and 20-11. The top and bottom of the curved trestle on which the harvest table sits. If you look carefully at the bottom piece shown in Illus. 20-11, you can see that it is glued up from several pieces rather than mortised in the usual way.

been cut in half and flipped over in order to alternate end grains. The top is in fact 93″ rather that 96″ long because Mader knew that to use the full 8′ length in the top, he'd have to use 10′ stock. You'll note that 4 pieces of 1 x 12 should add up to somewhere between 44″ and 46″ in width, depending on factors including drying and the scale in use at the time of sawing. Another ½″ was lost to ripping the boards. But that still leaves nearly 1′ of width that was consumed in the process of making the top a perfect glue job. Since the builder was, in effect, jointing with his table saw, he lost more than ¹⁄₃₂″ to ¹⁄₁₆″ per pass. Some builders with fully equipped workshops will say the process wasted nearly 8 board feet of lumber; others will say that the loss ratio falls within acceptable parameters. I was interested to note that I couldn't find all the seams in the finished top: the joints were that good. This attests to both the quality of the joining method and the advantages of gluing only two pieces of a panel at a time.

After the top was glued together, the glue squeeze-out was chipped away and the panel was flattened, first with a hand plane and then with a belt sander. The table top is deliberately less than perfectly flat, so it will mirror the real period

pieces. An interesting sidelight of this finishing process is Mader's personal project emblem; he lays a brass brad near the edge of the finished top, and strikes it with a hammer hard enough to make an indentation equal to about half the brad's thickness (Illus. 20-12). Then he fills the indentation with epoxy cement and drives the board the rest of the way home. After the glue has set, any section of the brad or glue that's sitting above the surface is ground away with the belt sander and polished with hand sanding. Details like this make all the difference between an acceptable project and an interesting one.

Retrospectively, the designer/builder wishes he had added another pair of stretchers to make the top more rigid. These pieces are shown as optional in the drawings.

After the top was sanded smooth, it was attached to the base with a number of table irons of the same variety used in my other projects (Illus. 20-13).

After completing the assembly, sand the unit smooth and finish it with Minwax Jacobean. The matching chairs shown in Illus. 20-1 were purchased at an unfinished store, and were finished at the same time. The result is a dining room set that in a furniture store would cost at least ten times what it took to make it. Additionally, the builder has a project of which he can be very proud. This value can't be measured in dollars.

Illus. 20-12 (above left). The brass nail inset in the corner is Mader's trademark.
Illus. 20-13 (above right). An inside view of the top shows several table irons holding the top to the leg set.

21.
Tiled Table

Commercially sold tiled tables are terribly expensive. The tiled table described and illustrated in this chapter (Illus. 21-1 and 21-2) is based, albeit loosely, on one we saw in a well-known discount furniture chain, priced at nearly $800. Our version cost well under $200, and is *far* nicer than the commercial product.

It's probably a good idea to buy your tile before you begin planning your table. At the store we shopped at, we found tile that ranged from 59¢ to $2.79 per piece. We bought 28 pieces of all-white 59¢ close-outs. We bought wavy-edged tiles, but you should use square-cornered tile. We also bought a gallon of tile cement, some grout, silicone seal, and a trowel.

All the tiled tables we've seen had the tiles arranged in four rows of seven tiles apiece, for a total of 28 pieces. This four by seven arrangement appears to make the best possible proportion for a rectangular table, so choose your tile by size as well as by color. There's no tile cutting required, so making the tiled table is *far* easier than tiling a floor or a countertop of predefined size. The size of tile indicates what the size of the table must be.

We bought commercial legs because that was

Illus. 21-1. Tiled table.

138

much quicker than trying to make shaped legs; I cut ¾″ from the end of each to allow for metal feet and the extra thickness of the top.

I cut pieces for the aprons and notched them 2¼″ from each end for the corner supports, which fastened to the legs with large bolts and to the aprons with screws. This will also permit removing the table's legs for easier shipping.

Then I laid out the curves for the apron (Illus. 21-3). Four inches from the ends I drew a line parallel to the end; 2½″ from the top I drew another line parallel to the top. At the centerline

Parts List for the Tiled Table (Excludes Tiles)

Label	Part	Quantity	Thickness	Width	Length
A	Legs (commercial pine)	4			
B	Short Apron	2	1″	4½″	29½″
C	Long Apron	2	1″	4½″	53½″
D	Particle-Core Top	1	¾″	35″	59″
E	Long Moulding	2	1⅛″	3¾″	63¼″
F	Short Moulding	2	1⅛″	3¾″	39¼″

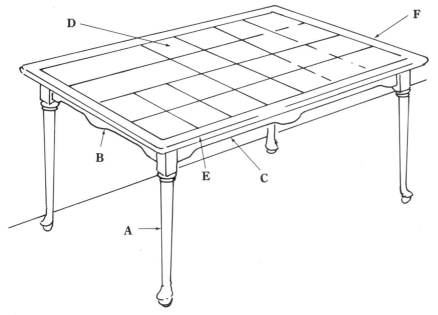

Illus. 21-2. Drawing of tiled table.

Illus. 21-3. The apron pieces laid out on the table-top, ready to be marked out.

2½" in diameter, and is ideal for these curves. The sanding needn't be perfect, but it should be thorough—after all, the piece will be routed half-round on both sides of this surface.

Many woodworkers advocate fancy jigs and fixtures for drum sanding. My method for doing this is much easier; I clamp an available piece of 2 x material at the end and cross-brace it to the drill-press table with a small thin piece of stock from my scrap bin (Illus. 21-7).

Routing each piece on both sides requires some clamping (Illus. 21-8). I still like to use the Elu 3304 router better than any other because it operates quietly and is small enough to fit around even clamped small pieces. Don't forget clamp pads; use them on the front and the back; if you

Illus. 21-4. The actual layout.

(27" from either end on the long apron or 15" on the short aprons) I added a ¾" segment of a circle. There are two arcs at either end. I made the first with the edge of a funnel (which had a 6¾" diameter), meeting both parallel lines; the second arc is made by having the funnel meet the first arc and the bottom edge (Illus. 21-4).

The pieces can be easily laid out and cut on a band saw (Illus. 21-5). I cut each laid-out piece, and then traced each onto its mate. Make sure the pieces match by sanding them together with a drum sander. The one shown in Illus. 21-6 is

Illus. 21-5. The layout on the band saw.

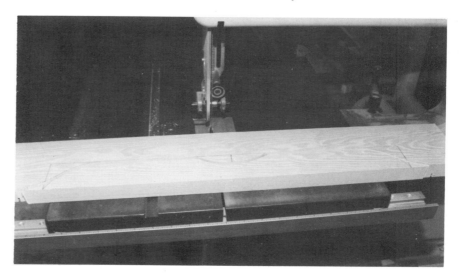

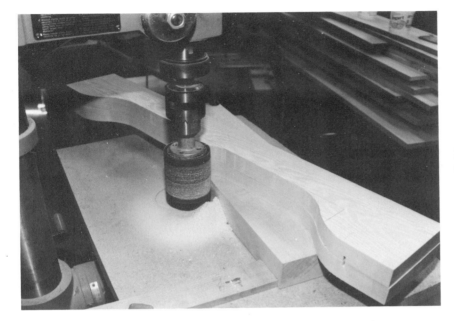

Illus. 21-6. Drum-sanding the long apron pieces.

Illus. 21-7. A view of the drum-sanding jig.

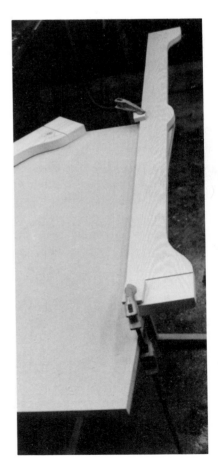

Illus. 21-8. The setup for rounding over the edges.

omit them on the back, you're likely to do so again on the front, and then you'll have a problem.

After the aprons have been shaped and sanded to your satisfaction, attach them to the legs; a pair of drills makes using the Vix-Bit® and the screwdriver easier (Illus. 21-9). The Makita driver accessory is almost a necessity if you want to use your slotted screws before converting to Phillips® or, preferably, square-drive screws.

Illus. 21-10. This large router facilitated running the bit to cut the curves on the moulding that will go around the tile.

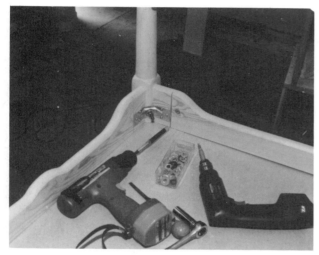

Illus. 21-9. A Vix-Bit® and power driver make installing corner brackets very easy.

After mounting the legs, you can cut slots for tabletop fasteners with your biscuit joiner; set the tool for biscuit size 0.

We laid the tile before attaching the edges, but this was a real mistake! Before you begin tiling the top, apply your edging material and finish the table (Illus. 21-10); only then should you begin mounting the tile. We trimmed 1¼"=thick ponderosa pine to 3¾" wide, and then used the CMT tabletop rounding bit on the top face of the material and a ⅜" radius corner-rounding bit on the bottom face; in a way, a larger round-over bit would have been preferable, even though that would have meant using an edge guide to keep the router square to the edge of the material. A 1⁹⁄₁₆" by ¾" rabbet was cut from the bottom face. After cutting the moulding to rough length, we did the final fitting using the Lion Miter Trimmer to en-

sure the best fits all the way around. The mitred corners were joined with glue and #20 joining biscuits, and the long edges were screwed into place, each in two places.

To finish the table, we applied two coats of white stain to give the table a "pickled" appearance, and we followed this with eight coats of Hydrocote® polyurethane varnish. After waiting several days for the final coat to dry, we applied painters' masking tape to the edges to keep from ruining our finished material with adhesive or grout.

Square-cornered tile will force you to be more professionally accurate—the wavy-edged tiles we used were very forgiving, allowing even the rankest of amateurs enough leeway to succeed. The manufacturer's directions for square-cornered tile almost seemed forbidding, because they go on for pages and look *so* complicated. But it's not that hard. Here's what we did: We drew a series of 8" x 8" grids on the table (Illus. 21-11). We found that we could see them through the cement, so the job was pretty easy. We started in the middle and worked towards the edges, knowing that if the first tile is laid square, the rest of the job will be simple. We scooped out the cement with a 3" putty knife (Illus. 21-12) and spread it with the recommended trowel, holding it at about a 60° angle (Illus. 21-13–21-15); the manufacturer's directions instructed us to form ridges and pull off the excess so it doesn't come out between the tile joints. We spread a generous amount of cement. The manufacturer's recommended spread rate is 20 to 30 square feet per gallon, and our 32″ x 56″ surface represented somewhere between 13–14 square feet, so we were right on target.

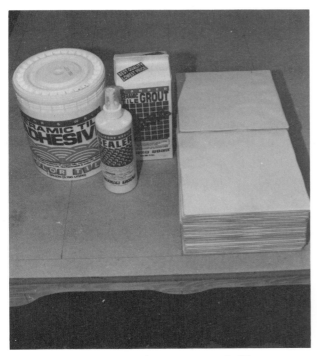

Illus. 21-11. Tile, adhesive, grout, and silicone sealer. Note the series of 8″ x 8″ grids that have been drawn on the table. Had I been smart, I'd have attached the moulding on the edges first.

Illus. 21-13. Beginning to spread the adhesive.

Illus. 21-12. Applying the adhesive to the tabletop.

Illus. 21-14. The spread adhesive should look something like this.

Illus. 21-15. Use a trowel at a 60° angle to spread the adhesive.

To add the tiles, do the following: twist each piece of tile into place rather than trying to slide it in (Illus. 21-16–21-21); apply enough downward pressure to ensure that the entire surface makes contact. Use equal pressure, to make sure the entire surface makes contact with the base. In an area as small as a table, you shouldn't have this problem, but if the cement starts to "skin" over, rework it with the trowel to ensure that fresh adhesive meets the tile. After the tiles have all been laid, make sure they are all about equal height, to prevent problems later, and then clean them (Illus. 21-22 and 21-23). Allow the adhesive to set 24 hours before applying the grout.

Grout comes in a whole rainbow of colors; perhaps we were being cowardly when we chose

Illus. 21-16. Pressing the first piece into place.

Illus. 21-17. Applying the fifth piece.

Illus. 21-18. Spreading more cement.

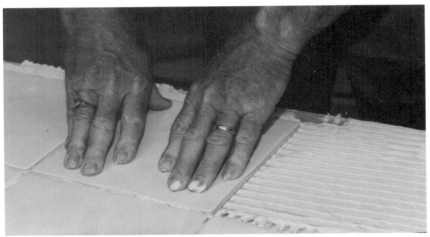

Illus. 21-19. "Wiggle" the tile onto the cement. This helps to seat it firmly into the cement.

Illus. 21-20. Cleaning up the edge.

Illus. 21-21. Laying the last of the tiles.

Illus. 21-23. Clean up the tile with 3M Scotch-Brite® and a solution of mild household cleaner.

Illus. 21-22. Put a layer of plastic wrap over the cement before putting the lid on it, to preserve it for another time.

white. Whatever color you choose, mix the grout according to the manufacturer's directions, and then spread it around with an old window-washing squeegee or a Sheetrock spoon (Illus. 21-24–21-29). Wipe off as much excess grout as possible, but be sure to go over the entire area at least three or four times—always on the diagonal to the tiles. Be sure to fill all the grout joints all the way to the top; the tile manufacturer cautioned us that exposed edges on ceramic tile can chip or wear prematurely. Sealing the grout lines from dirt, moisture, and mildew is accomplished by applying two coats of grout sealer after the grout has cured at least 72 hours.

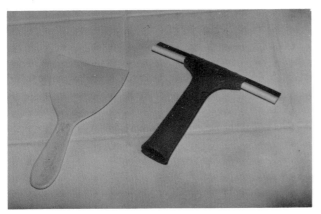

Illus. 21-24. The tools used to apply the grout. On the left is a Sheetrock spoon. On the right is a squeegee.

Illus. 21-25. The texture of the mixed grout. An ice-cream bucket is the ideal container for this material.

Illus. 21-26. Spreading the grout with the Sheetrock spoon.

Illus. 21-27. By the time the grout is completely spread, the project looks like a complete mess!

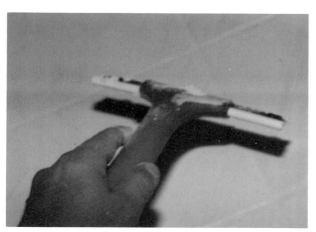

Illus. 21-28. Run the squeegee at a diagonal to the joints in the tile.

Illus. 21-29. By the time the grout is spread, there's a lot of material left, and it is time to clean up the tools. If the tools aren't cleaned, they will be a total loss.

22.
Square-Based Round Table

When making a round table (22-1 and 22-2), it's nearly always a good idea to use a square base, particularly if the table is to be used for eating. Since one doesn't always have a cutting list to work from, one might calculate the length of the apron pieces in the square-based table by working *rearwards* through the formula for the hypotenuse of a right triangle, which is $\sqrt{A^2 + B^2}$.

There are several things that we know that can make it easier to compute the length of the apron pieces. For instance, we have established that the apron/base is square; so, for the sake of this calculation, $A = B$. Thus, if we know the diameter of the table, we can square that, and then take the square root of ½ that square for the total possible hypotenuse. Further, we should know how much overhang is needed, and how thick the legs will be. These dimensions must be subtracted from that total, to reach the apron length.

Here's an example: If I am making a 42″-diameter table with 1⅞″ thick legs, I multiply 42 x 42, which equals 1,764. Then, I divide by two, since the sides are equal. 1,764 divided by 2 equals 882.

Next, I take the square root of 882. Use a calculator if you have one. The square root of 882 is 29.7. Then I subtract the minimum acceptable overhang from each side. Since the minimum acceptable overhang is 2″ and there are two sides, that gives me a total of 4″. Four subtracted from 29.7 is 25.7.

Next, I subtract the thickness of *both* legs: 1⅞″

x 2 = 3.75″. I round 3.75″ to 3.7″ and subtract it from 25.7, which is 22″. With these calculations, I have determined I will be using four 22″ apron pieces.

To calculate the size of the table with the apron slats as the given, simply do the following: add the apron length (let's say 30″) plus the thickness of

Illus. 22-1. A round table, designed as an eating table to be used in a screened-in porch. Also see Illus. 22-2.

149

Parts List for the Square-Based Round Table

Label	Part	Quantity	Thickness	Width	Length
A	Top*	1	¾″		
B	Apron	4	¾″	3″	22″
C	Leg	4	1⅞″	1⅞″	28¼″

*The top is 44″ in diameter.

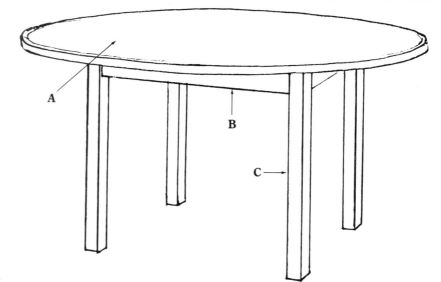

Illus. 22-2. Assembly drawing of round table.

both legs (let's say 2″ each) plus the minimum overhang (let's call it a generous 4″). Square this figure, multiply it by 2, and divide the resulting figure by 50. This will yield a base of almost 51″.

If you are going to use fancy legs, you might try using a base made of construction-grade wood rather than fancy or exotic materials.

The table described and illustrated in this chapter is designed as an eating table for a screened-in porch area that is used only part of the year. It is also designed to be easy to transport, so we're using steel corner braces with wing nuts and hanger bolts. Woodcraft's corner braces are more substantial than others I have seen because they require six screws be driven into the aprons at each corner rather than the more usual one. To install these braces, a ³⁄₃₂″-wide, ¼″-deep saw kerf should be cut parallel to each leg, although most saws

After the slots were cut, I inserted the corner

cut a ⅛″ kerf, which is perfectly acceptable. I cut these kerfs about 2½″ from the ends, though you might want to vary that distance based on the thickness of your table's legs. If these slots are to be cut in apron pieces of different lengths or if you don't have a length-setting stop on your cros-scut gauge, you might use a mock fence to set the distance accurately for these repeated cuts. brackets into the slots and drilled pilot holes for the screws. If you are making more than one table base at a time, you may want to use a self-centering drill bit and a power screwdriver.

Drilling the legs for the hanger bolts can be done freehand, or it can be more squarely done in a V-block on the drill press. Drill the holes 1½″ from the top on the inside corner of the leg.

After the legs have been drilled for the hanger bolts, the hanger bolts can be attached with a nut driver by simply applying a cap nut to the bolt-end of the nut (Illus 22-3 and 22-4); if you can find steel cap nuts, they'll be less likely to break under repeated use than are the more readily available (and more expensive) brass cap nuts.

Illus. 22-3 and 22-4. Put the hanger bolts into the legs with cap nuts or a pair of jammed nuts.

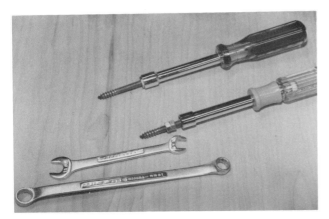

Illus. 22-4.

Attach all four legs to the apron with wing nuts. Though I had done everything in my power to ensure a square setup, I wasn't totally satisfied that the table base was completely flat before I fastened the top. It seems to me that I'm using the top of this table to ensure the flatness of the rest of the work.

For this table I cut the round top from a half sheet of ApplePly® veneer-core maple plywood (Illus. 22-5) because I knew that this material's edges would be good enough to keep, and that the table would have a tablecloth on it nearly all the time anyway.

The steps in making the top consisted of drawing and cutting the circle. I drilled a pair of holes in a stick 21″ apart to hold a very sharp awl at one end and a pencil at the other. I stuck the awl into the wood, scribed the circle, and then cut out the circle freehand with a sabre saw, carefully staying about ⅛″ outside the line.

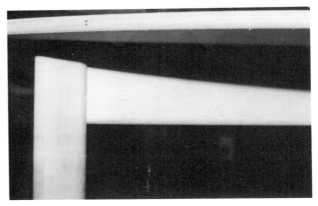

Illus. 22-5. This view of the tabletop's edge shows one of the voids (just above the apron/leg joint) in the supposedly void-free Apply-ply.®

Then I adjusted the trammel point to hold the router. Since I was making a single round table, I simply clamped a piece to the trammel to hold the router at the appropriate distance from the center (Illus. 22-6 and 22-7); then I held the router

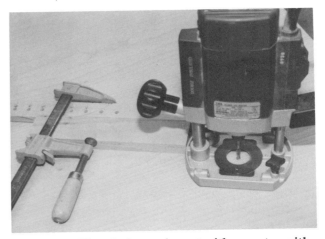

Illus. 22-6. The circle can be cut with a router with a spiral bit that is simply held against a shop-made trammel point at the proper distance from the circle's center. Cutting this circle is far easier than one might suspect.

Illus. 22-7. Using a spiral bit like the one shown here gives much better results when cutting than does using a regular straight blade bit.

by one handle, and the trammel and the router base with the other, and made about four passes around the top, each pass cutting the circle a bit deeper. The jig shown in Illus. 22-6 and 22-7 is good enough for a single circle, but if you're going to make more than one, you're sure to want something a bit more elaborate which attaches the router to the trammel, perhaps using the router's guide holes as attaching points. Make such a jig as simple as possible.

After the circle was cut out, I rounded over the edge at *both* faces with a 3/16″ round-over bit. I had toyed with the idea of using a fancier edge to complement the decorative quality of this many-ply plywood, but the rounding-over proved to be simpler to do. Next, I attached the leg, apron, and top (Illus. 22-8 and 22-9).

Illus. 22-8 and 22-9. Two views of the led/apron/top assembly. Illus. 22-9 is a closeup that shows the legs attached with corner irons and wing nuts, and the table fasteners positioned near the corners.

Illus. 22-9.

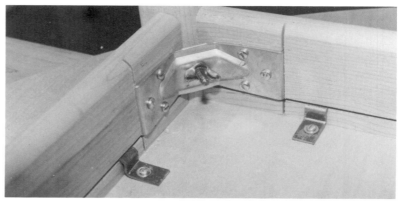

Finally, I put a bit of putty in one of the voids in the plywood and proceeded to sand the piece. After completing the sanding, I used Minwax® Jacobean oil finish, which I followed a couple of days later with three or four coats of Hydrocote® polyurethane.

When the table is shown in its natural setting, without a tablecloth, you'll note that these finishes do provide a handsome finish (Illus. 22-10).

Illus. 22-10. The unfinished table in my shop. A table like this can be fabricated in a very short time.

23.
Card Table

A table that folds out of the way is particularly handy, but the card tables one can find in the stores are either too flimsy or too expensive to be practical for most people. The 60-plus-year-old table that served as a model for the table described and illustrated here (Illus. 23-1–23-4) is a solution to the problem of the portable table. This table has seen regular use for a very long time, and while its varnish is beginning to fade a bit, and the glue joints on the top are beginning to separate on the ends, the table is still functional. Besides, it could be built in a variety of ways, as complicated or as simple, as inexpensive or luxurious, as the builder might want.

The top of the original table is made of glued-up maple or birch, although the table illustrated here is made of cherry. A woodworker who wants to build a fancier table might prefer walnut or mahogany. Since the piece will use only about 6 board feet, this won't add much more to the cost of the table. The top has a nice "classical"-style moulding planed (or, more modernly, routed) all the way around. A purely utilitarian top might be nicely made with Baltic birch plywood.

The legs of the table illustrated here are made of the same material as the top; these legs are configured in a traditional Early-American style (Illus. 23-5–23-8). A turning of your own design would be just as fine, or, if you haven't a lathe, straight, square legs or gently tapered legs would also be handsome.

The battens at the outside edge of the legs were each applied to the table illustrated here with three countersunk wood screws, one in each board of the top; this fastening method may have contributed to the slight splitting of the top over the years. Two screws per board, one near either end, would be sufficient. These pieces are probably

Illus. 23-1. Cherry card table.

154

Parts List for the Card Table

Label	Part	Quantity	Thickness	Width	Length
A	Top	1	$3/4''$	$24\frac{1}{4}''$	$33''$
B	Leg	4	$1\frac{5}{8}''$	$1\frac{5}{8}''$	$26\frac{5}{8}''$
C	End Rail	2	$2\frac{7}{8}''$	$7\frac{1}{2}''$	$22\frac{3}{8}''$
D	Apron	2	$3/4''$	$3''$	$20''$
E	Center Block for Holdfast	1	$13/16''$	$2''$	$5''$
F	Holdfast	1	$5/16''$	$2''$	$27\frac{1}{2}''$
G	Square Hinges	4	$1\frac{1}{4}''$		

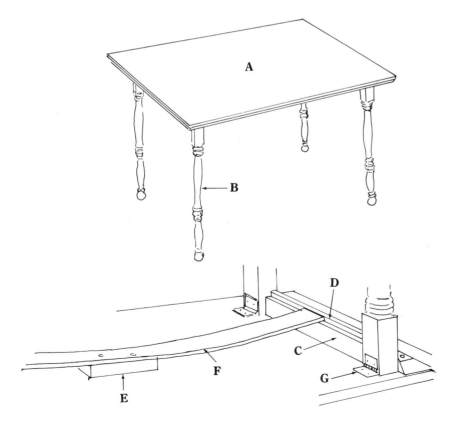

Illus. 23-2. Drawings of the cherry table and its underside.

Illus. 23-3. The underside of the
original cherry table.

Illus. 23-4. The cherry table
folded up, ready to go.

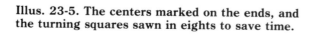

Illus. 23-5. The centers marked on the ends, and
the turning squares sawn in eights to save time.

Illus. 23-6. Laying out for the lathe work.

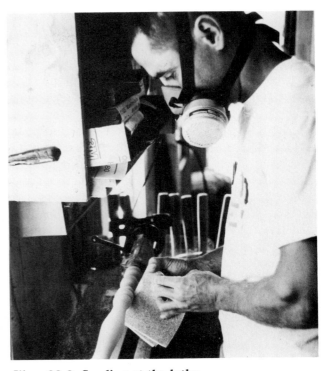

Illus. 23-8. Sanding at the lathe.

Illus. 23-7. Turning at the lathe.

Illus. 23-9. Mortising one leg.

best attached after the legs and the holdfast have been mounted.

The aprons have a ¼″ deep x ⅜″ wide rabbet along the bottom inside edge and a ¼″ thick x ¾″ wide, perfectly centered tenon on either end. The corresponding mortises on the table's legs were let in with a circular saw, but that leaves just over 2″ of useless slot showing; surely you can let in your mortises more neatly than this, either with mortising chisels or a (router-) powered mortiser (Illus. 23-9). After you have cut both mortises and tenons, the pairs of legs can be glued to the aprons. Alternatively, this is an almost ideal application for your plate joiner.

The 2″ x 5″ center block is glued lengthwise to the underside of the top. The piece of ⁵⁄₁₆″ holdfast (Illus. 23-10) should be made of ash or some other springy stock. Illus 23-11 shows how over the years this piece has taken on a bowed form. With two substantial screws (say, 1½″ x #10), attach this to the center block, centering it as precisely as possible. Then set the rabbetted faces of the leg aprons into position at the ends of the holdfast, and screw the hinges into place. The last step of assembly is to screw the battens into place just as close as possible to the fully extended legs. The legs can be folded after lifting the holdfast slightly. Work the mechanism a few times to wear it into place, and then sand and finish per the finishing schedule that most suits your fancy.

Chances are, making just one of these tables would be a mistake, for it is sure to be popular wherever you use it; this and a couple of director's chairs would make elegant furnishings for even a picnic.

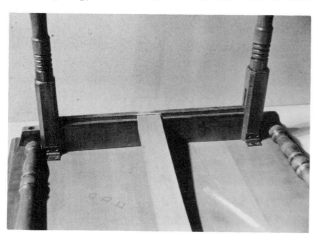

Illus. 23-10. A closeup of one leg set being braced in place by the springy center.

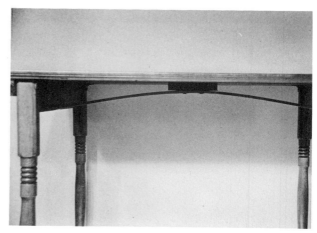

Illus. 23-11. An underside view of the spring mechanism holding the legs in place.

24.
Decorative Planter

This project (Illus. 24-1–24-3) was probably my first attempt at "serious" woodworking when I made it two decades or so ago. My wife had shown me a similar, but rather more ornate, planter in some magazine, and I decided to make this one for her as a present. As I drew my plans, my goals were to design a planter simple enough that I could build with the machinery I had at hand (which consisted of a small radial arm saw and a variety of hand tools) and with a limited amount of skill.

Now, nearly two decades later, the piece still looks pretty good, and, more importantly, its structural integrity is beyond question. It has functioned over the years as both a dirt-in planter and as a receptacle for various flower pots, for both displaying and propagating plants. As it is designed, the unit is large enough that a light fixture could be hung under the main surface so that another "row" of plants could be grown below. Alternatively, one might alter the unit so that it would better match your window size or other decorating needs.

After thinking about your objectives in building the unit, you can begin planning its construction. The first step in the construction is to order or build your pan. I suggest you have yours fabricated at a sheet-metal shop; most hobbyist woodworkers lack both the tools and the metalworking skills to get this right. I had my pan fabricated of heavy-gauge sheet copper and soldered corners because someone suggested that over time a galvanized

Illus. 24-1. Decorative planter. Also see page D of the color section.

pan might rust; besides, the copper has become ever more beautiful as it has aged. The corners are all double-thick, and there is a ½″ or so of material folded back all the way around the top. There is probably enough strength in the pan itself that some of the steps I took to support it weren't needed. While your pan is being made, you can determine what wood you want and start making a cutting list. To reproduce my unit exactly, all you have to do is follow my cutting list.

As noted above, the joinery is fairly simple. First, assemble the frame for the metal pan. Pieces A and B as indicated in Illus. 24-2 are mitred. The mitres were cut on the radial arm saw. Rabbets ½″ x 1″ were cut at what will be the bottom of each piece. Today, I'd biscuit these

joints together, but when the unit was built, they were probably glued and screwed, since the ends of the mitres aren't visible anyway.

Next, cut the 2″ x 2″ legs which are part C in Illus. 24-2. At one end of each leg cut a 1″ deep x 4″ long notch; the mitred assembly described in the previous paragraph will rest in (and be fastened to) these notches. In the same plane as this first set of notches, cut a 1″-deep and 2″-long notch 2″ from the bottom (or 6″ from the bottom if it's important that you get a vacuum cleaner under it regularly); this set of notches supports the lower shelf. These notches can be cut with repeated passes of the blade on either a table or radial saw.

Parts List for the Decorative Planter*

Label	Part	Quantity	Thickness	Width	Length
A	Mitred End for Frame	2	$^{13}/_{16}$″	4″	$17^{7}/_{8}$″
B	Mitred Front and Rear for Frame	2	$^{13}/_{16}$″	4″	$45^{5}/_{8}$″
C	Legs	4	$1^{3}/_{4}$″	$1^{3}/_{4}$″	$25^{1}/_{4}$″
D	Plywood Shelf	1	$^{3}/_{4}$″	$16^{7}/_{8}$″	$44^{5}/_{8}$″
E	Shelf Front and Rear Caps	2	$^{13}/_{16}$″	2″	$45^{5}/_{8}$″
F	Shelf End Caps	2	$^{13}/_{16}$″	2″	$17^{5}/_{8}$″
G	Masonite®	1	$^{1}/_{8}$″	16″	44″
H	Brace for G	2	$^{3}/_{4}$″	1″	44″
I	Brace for G	2	$^{1}/_{2}$″	$2^{1}/_{2}$″	16″
J	Fabricated Pan	1	3″ deep	16″	44″

*Though Philippine mahogany was used on the project illustrated and described here, you should use any material that suits your purposes.

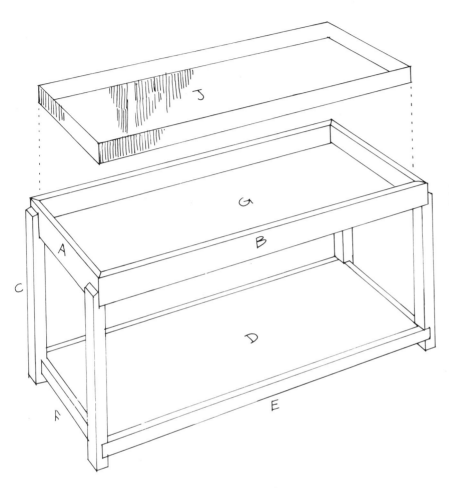

Illus. 24-2. **Assembly drawing of decorative planter.**

Then cut pieces E and F, mitre them at their ends with ¾" x ½" rabbets at what will be the top. Assemble this frame as you did the frame for the pan above. The plywood shelf (piece D) should drop right into this frame.

Next, screw both frame assemblies into the notches on the legs, using 1¼" flathead wood screws. Then, with the assembly upside-down, screw pieces H and I into the rabbets on the top frame. I used two 1¼" x #8 flathead wood screws in each piece H and five on each piece I, two of which went through H as well.

Next, stand the unit up. Insert a piece of ⅛" Masonite into the bottom of the pan frame and a piece of ¾" plywood into the lower shelf frame.

Set the sheet-metal pan in place; screw it in with three like-metal sheet-metal screws on each long side.

Finish-sand the unit, and then apply the finish of your choice. Since Hydrocote polyurethane is both easy to apply and rated strong enough for gym floors, it is definitely worth your consideration; it's what I'd use were I making the project today.

Many of the techniques I'd use to build this project today either didn't exist then or weren't available to me. While some of the fastening methods I used on the table strike me today as a little crude, there's no question but that the project has continued to work for many years.

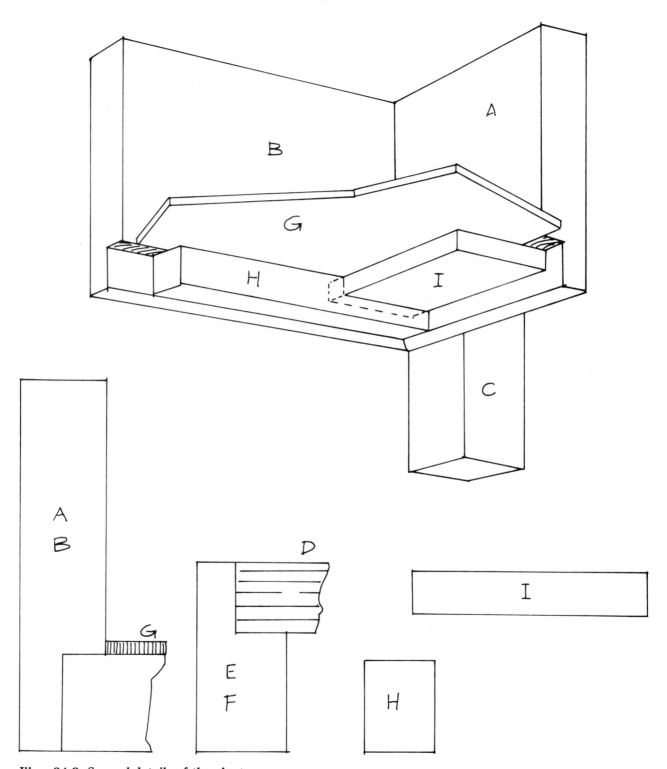

Illus. 24-3. Several details of the planter.

25.
Plant Stand/Low Table/Bench

This attractive plant stand (Illus. 25-1 and 25-2) looks great with furniture of almost any style. It provides you with the opportunity to make a wide variety of joints while spending very little on material. There are basically only five pieces in the entire project.

Glue up and then cut piece A to size. The hand-hold in the middle is optional, but might be useful; I make one of these by drilling a pair of 1⅛″ holes about 3″ apart on center (Illus. 25-3), and then cutting out the piece between them with a sabre saw, controlling the cut so it will be as straight as possible. A bit of filing makes this hole ready for the round-over edge treatment that the sides get. Of course, this operation might be done more quickly and accurately with a router and an edge guide. After sanding the top, round the edges of the top and of the handhold with a ³⁄₁₆″ round-over router bit.

Before you even start tapering the pieces B and C for the sides, cut them to length and cut their curves out. I laid out a 7″ circle 5½″ from the bottom of the pieces, but you may want to adjust this shape. The amount of the circle that remains at the bottom may be too much to suit you. Remove stock from the bottoms to suit your taste. Leaving some concavity here adds to this project's aura of mystery after it has been completed. Scalloping or rounding over these edges is optional; I

Illus. 25-1. Plant stand/low table/bench.

163

Parts List for the Plant Stand/Low Table/Bench

Label	Part	Quantity	Thickness	Width	Length
A	Top	1	1″	12½″	12½″
B	Side	2	1″	12″	20″
C	Side	2	1″	10½″	20″
D	Attaching Block	2			

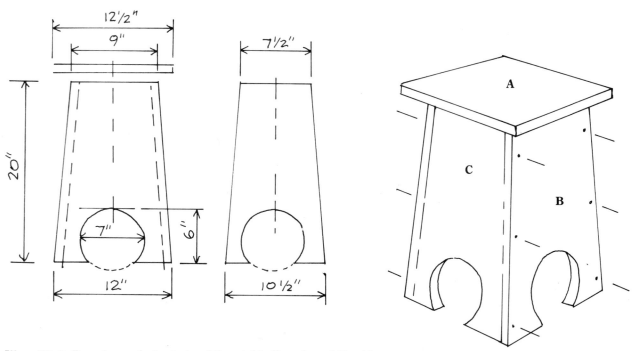

Illus. 25-2. Drawings of plant stand/low table/bench and its sides.

prefer to leave the cut as nearly square-edged as I can, so I round these corners with a ³⁄₁₆″ round-over bit.

Rout out these part circles with a small trammel point (Illus. 25-4–25-6). The one shown in Illus. 25-5 was standard equipment with the Elu 3304 router kit. A spiral router bit permitted disc removal in only two revolutions around the point. I found it was better to start the cut nearer the top than the bottom of the circle, so that as much

of the router as possible would be supported when the piece to which the trammel point is "attached" drops out.

I used a 1⅛″ outside diameter washer to mark the sharp corners for scroll-sawing and sanding. This left an attractive continuous edge for rounding over inside and out. Do this now with a ³⁄₈″ round-over bit.

Cut pieces B and C. If you're feeling adventur-ous, cut four of pieces B instead of two each of B

Illus. 25-3. Drilling the 1⅛″ holes on 3″ centers is a good way to start cutting the handhold in the top. Cut this handhold only if you'll use the project more as a bench than as a table.

Illus. 25-5. A view of the router/trammel setup for removing the circle from the center.

Illus. 25-4. Here's a side of the base with the circle scribed for the leg cutout; note the use of the Record holdfast to keep the work firm. Lacking this facility on your workbench, be sure to put some scrap stock down so that you don't ruin the tabletop as you rout through the material.

Illus. 25-6. Here a side of the table is mounted on the bench. The large circle has been routed out, but the corners left haven't been rounded over.

and C. As you cut the width down to 9″ by taking 1½″ of taper off each side, mitre the cuts so that the table may be assembled seamlessly. You'll have to cut very squarely to your line, or these long mitres will have ugly gaps in them. If you mitre them successfully, you'll be ready to biscuit-join the edges.

If you are working according to the cutting list, cut pieces B with a 1½″ taper; then cut pieces C with a 2¼″ taper. Before assembling the pieces, use piece C to lay out the lines on pieces B that will make them parallel to the ground as they taper; set your saw to this angle, and, with a fine-cutting blade, cut both the tops and bottoms so they will be square to the ground. This will be approximately 4–5° from true square, but you should check this against your actual parts. I do this by setting the fence for the length of the piece to be tapered, setting the blade to the desired angle, and then cutting both ends without changing the fence setting; there is only a very light cut taken off either side.

Glue and screw pieces B to the edges of pieces C. Be sure to countersink and cap your screws; it would be more decorative—and certainly as strong—to biscuit-join these joints instead of screwing them together (Illus 25-7). Three biscuits in each corner do wonders for both alignment and strength of the joints; additionally, they eliminate any need for the glue blocks described a couple of paragraphs hence.

If you assemble the piece as I have, you'll find that rounding over the corners with a large diameter (say, ¾″) router bit eliminates the appearance of inferior-looking joinery.

If you'll use this as a bench rather than as a plant stand or table, glue glue blocks inside your joints for strength (Illus. 25-8). Not only are glue blocks good for reinforcing joints in repair work, but they also do an admirable job of stiffening up joints in out-of-the-way parts of new work. The best way to get glue blocks is probably to make them of scrap stock; I regularly make strips that are ¾″ x ¾″ + the hypotenuse from routine shop rippings that might otherwise just feed the fire-

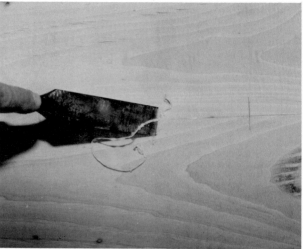

Illus. 25-7. Since each side of the base had to be glued up, I glued with biscuits at the center of each piece. Here the glue squeeze-out is being removed before the surface is sanded.

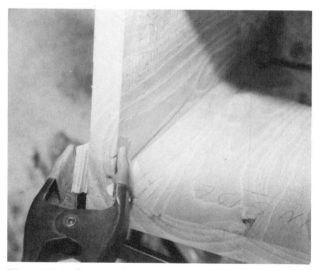

Illus. 25-8. Spring clamps are enough to hold the glue blocks in place.

place; I set these in a corner for cutting into glue blocks of whatever length a project requires. Using them doesn't take much extra time, and they help to make our assemblies more rigid.

Attach the top by screwing through attaching blocks made from the cutouts (Illus. 25-9); these blocks slide into slots made with your biscuit joiner, and screw to the top. I did this even though it is hard to beat table fasteners like Woodworker's Store fasteners for price, ease of use, quickness, and maybe even appearance.

If you have thoroughly sanded all the pieces as you assembled them, all you should need now is a light hand sanding and some finishing. Ordinarily, I'd suggest that projects not be stained (Illus. 25-10 and 25-11). I originally thought that this piece should be stained dark. Now that I've given it several coats of Minwax Jacobean finish, I'm not so sure! I'd be inclined to make these small tables of ebony or teak if I could afford to. Apply your stain coat; then, if the table is to be used as a planter, make it just as waterproof as you can so that it will remain beautiful for a long time. Epoxy finish is recommended if this table is to have lots of use with plants.

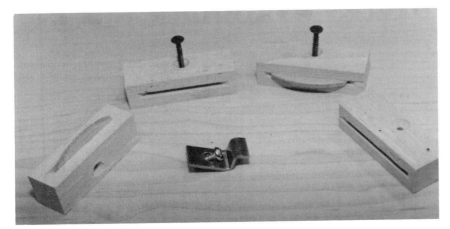

Illus. 25-9. This type of table fastener can be fabricated readily enough in the shop, but it's not really much of a substitute for the Woodworker's Store fasteners.

Illus. 25-10. A view of the completed table on the workbench, before application of stain.

Illus. 25-11. The table with wet, glossy stain; this is still a long way from "finished."

26.
Gate-Leg Table

This is an ideal project for even novice turners, because there are many spindle parts, but they aren't very complicated. The original table shown in Illus. 26-1 and Illus. 26-2 may be as much as 100 years old. It has seen a considerable amount of use and has several features that are worth noting. First, the top is made of lumber-core plywood. Illus. 26-6 shows some damage it sustained over the years. Also, note the top is mounted to the aprons with pocket screws (Illus. 26-7 and 26-8), which many woodworkers think aren't sufficiently strong or traditional, a false assumption.

And, as Illus. 26-9 shows, a "modern" machined joint connects the drawer front to its sides.

The hinges that connect the gate legs to the body of the table are mortised in place with a double-deep mortise in the leg (Illus. 26-10 and 26-11). It wouldn't be imperative to make this mortise, but it does help to ensure a nice flush fit.

You can make this table with or without the radius rule joints by altering the hinge style. Frankly, though, the rule joint is much more attractive if made with ½″ cove and round-over bits. The drop-leaf hinges are mounted in 2½″-long

Illus. 26-1 (above left). A view of the gate-leg table as it sits every day. Illus. 26-2 (above right). The gate-leg table with both leaves up. Also see Illus. 26-3 and 26-4 and page G of the color section.

channels, the center of which is ½" from the edge of the body. As always, the longer part of the hinge goes on the leaf.

You can make a table like this with or without the elliptical top. You can make it with straight legs rather than the turned legs shown here, or you can design different legs by using a device like the Sears Router-Crafter to shape the stock which will become the legs (Illus. 26-12).

Parts List for the Gate-Leg Table on Page 170

Label	Part	Quantity	Thickness	Width	Length
A	Leg	8	1⅝"	1⅝"	28½"
B	Gate-Leg Spindle*	4	1⅝"	1⅝"	9½"
C	Short Spindle*	2	1⅝"	1⅝"	9½"
D	Long Spindle*	2	1⅝"	1⅝"	25⅛"
E	Top	1	¾"	14¼"	33½"
F	Drop Leaf	2	¾"	14¼"	33½"
G	Apron	2	13/16"	2⅞"	28⅛"
H	Short Apron	1	13/16"	2 13/16"	9½"
I	Apron Bottom	2	¾"	7½"	9½"
J	Drawer Side	2	½"	2⅞"	19½"
K	Drawer Back	1	½"	2¼"	7½"
L	Drawer Bottom	1	¼"	7¾"	15"
M	Drawer Front	1	¾"	2¾"	9 7/16"
N	Knob	1			
O	Table Hinges	3 pairs			
P	Hinges	2 pairs		2"	1⅝"

*Note: Tenon lengths have not been included, so add ¾" to either end for tenons. Make them as large in diameter as your equipment can machine them.

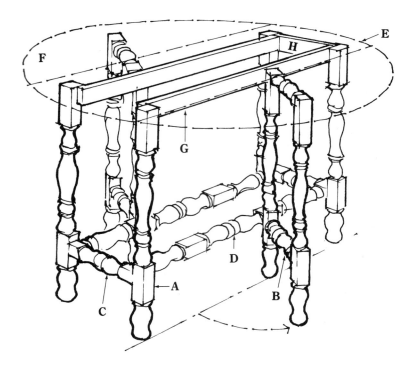

Illus. 26-3. Drawing of gate-leg table. Note that some of the parts identified in the parts list are not shown here.

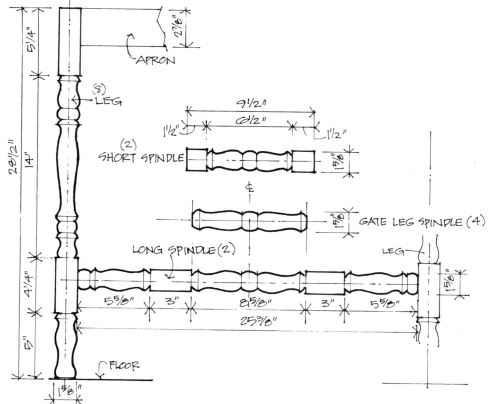

Illus. 26-4. Parts of the gate-leg table.

Illus. 26-5. The drop-leaf joint.

Illus. 26-6. The damaged corner that illustrates the plywood construction. This table, used since probably the turn of the century, has not been treated like an antique.

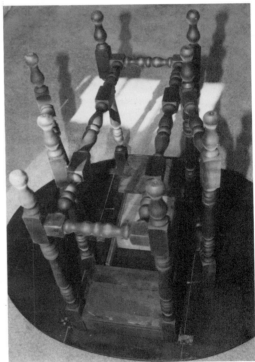

Illus. 26-8. Note that the aprons have a wide bottom which also serves as the drawer glide. This works surprisingly well.

Illus. 26-7. Mounting the table irons in a channel on the underside. Note the pocket-hole joint that mounts the apron to the top.

Illus. 26-9. Note the "modern" machined joint that connects the drawer front to its sides.

Illus. 26-10. The hinges that operate the gate leg are mortised into the leg.

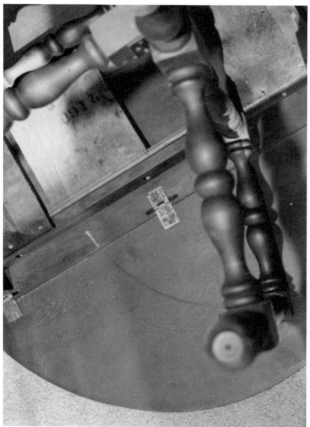

Illus. 26-11. Note the sweep where the gate leg has been opened over the years.

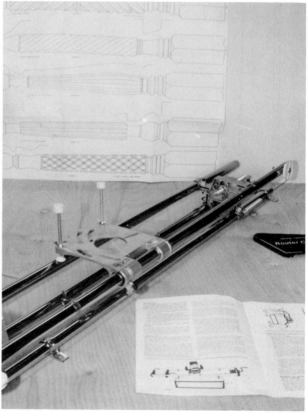

Illus. 26-12. The Sears Router Crafter comes with some suggested patterns for leg sets and an excellent instruction manual.

27.
Table Used Behind a Couch

The table described here is a long, narrow hall-type table, suitable for use behind a couch. Of course, most of the time when we hear about a behind-the-couch table, we're thinking about a couch whose back faces into the room rather than against a wall. If the table faces back into the room, it might be desirable to have a shelf or two under the top, but at what point does it then cease to be a table and become a bookcase?

The table described and illustrated here does not have shelves. We built two of these tables with two different sets of legs: one set 32″ long, the other 25″ long. Illus. 27-1 and 27-2 show these tables. These illustrations and Illus. 27-3 will prove instructive as you plan your own similar table.

This tall, narrow table is sufficiently graceful that it would handsomely adorn many rooms.

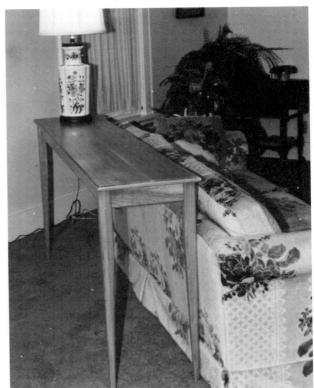

Illus. 27-1. The table behind this couch has the shorter of the leg sets.

Illus. 27-2. The table behind this couch has the longer leg set. Note that when used against the wall, the table with the longer leg set seemed to be preferred.

Parts List for the Couch Table

Label	Part	Quantity	Thickness	Width	Length
A	Top*	1	¾″	15″	70″
B	Leg**	4	1¾″	1¾″	24¼″
B	Alternate Leg	4	1¾″	1¾″	32″
C	Short Apron Piece	2	¾″	3″	10½″
D	Long Apron Piece	2	¾″	3″	64″

*Glued up from pieces not over 6″ wide.
**Either set of legs should be tapered, beginning 6″ from the top, to ¾″ x ¾″.

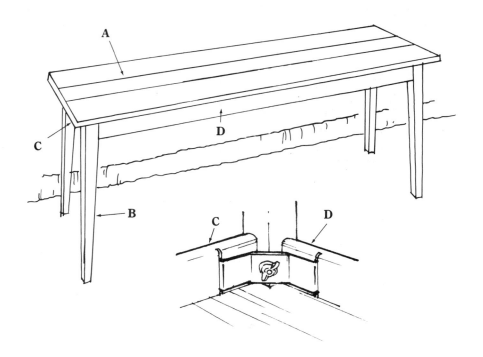

Illus. 27-3. Drawing of couch table.

Make it of fine wood. Working with good stock in an organized shop will save a great deal of time. I cut the legs from 2″ stock, tapered them on two sides, and rounded them over on all edges with a ½″ round-over bit. With a bit of practice and the right bit in your router table, this becomes a very fast operation.

Building this table is a simple matter of cutting,

shaping, sanding, and assembling the pieces (Illus. 27-4). Since there are only four apron pieces, four legs, and a top, the assembly could hardly be easier.

Since there are two sets of legs involved, I used ⁵⁄₁₆″ hanger bolts and wing nuts along with the Woodcraft Supply corner irons for the assembly (Illus. 27-5 and 27-6). By judiciously spacing the saw kerf that the corner irons ride in, we can determine how much offset from the front of the leg there will be. After studying the options, I determined that I would cut these kerfs 2¼″ from the ends of the apron pieces, even though this meant that I would have to space the wing nuts with four washers. These spacers appear to have no effect whatever on the strength of the assembly.

Illus. 27-4. You're likely to use the full length of your workbench when you build a table for behind a couch.

Illus. 27-5. This underside of the table shows the working of the Woodcraft corner set when used with wing nuts. Near the corner is a metal tabletop fastener.

Illus. 27-6. One does not need to be terribly strong to tighten the wing nuts tight enough to hold the legs in place.

28.
Split-Top Sofa Table

Commercial sofa or hall tables are generally expensive and not very graceful looking. We altered the dimensions of the usual sofa table to create this lovely, diminutive, and relatively inexpensive table (Illus. 28-1–28-3). This table is 54″ long, 29″ high, and 14″ deep. Many designers use this length and a 26″ height with an 18″ width, leaving themselves (or their customers) with a table that takes up too much space in small modern rooms and has an overall "clunky" appearance.

Actually, this project is based on an excellent but rather complicated design by Doug Haley. He had a lovely piece of stock that was wider but shorter than needed for his sofa table; when a customer insisted upon *this* piece of stock for the top, he sketched her this version—then he built it for her. His version included a pair of drawers, but I've omitted them here so the project can easily be completed in a weekend.

The table illustrated has cherry for the base and bird's-eye maple for the top, although the sizes will be accurate no matter which materials you choose. Here's how to make the project in a single weekend: Cut four apron pieces: two at ¾″ x 4″ x 8″ and two at ¾″ x 4″ x 48″. Then cut four legs 1¾″ x 1¾″ x 28¼″ (Illus. 28-4). Taper the legs

Illus. 28-1 and 28-2. Two settings for the split-top table. Here it is being used against a wall.

Illus. 28-2. Here the split-top table is being used behind a sofa.

Parts List for the Split-Top Sofa Table

Label	Part	Quantity	Thickness	Width	Length
A	Leg	4	1¾″	1¾″	28¼″
B	Short Apron	2	¾″	4″	8″
C	Long Apron	2	¾″	4″	48″
D	Top	3	¾″	14″	18″
E	Cross Pieces Attached to Ends of Middle Top	2	¾″	1¾″	10⁵/₁₆″
	Corner Brace	4			
	Biscuits				
	Tabletop Fastener				

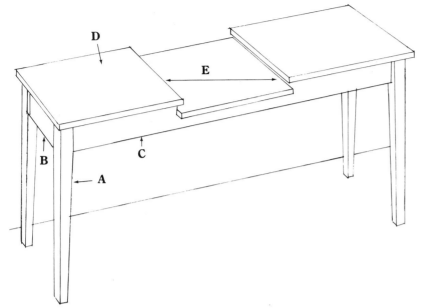

Illus. 28-3. Drawing of the split-top table.

Illus. 28-4. This layout of the legs helps to ensure that you cut the tapers on the right faces.

Illus. 28-5. A chisel plane is ideal for cleaning up this freshly sawn area.

with a shop-made taper jig. After tapering, the small end of the leg is 1 x 1″. Save the tapered cutoffs; they make useful shims for various projects around the house. As Illus. 28-5 shows, cutting tapers leave faces on the stock that need to be cleaned up; purists will use a hand plane or a scraper, but the rest of us will probably use a power sander.

All four lengths of each leg can be rounded over before the stock is cleaned up. This can be done with a router, but it can be done even better with a router table. While you have the round-over bit set up in the router, this might also be a good time to round over both sides of one edge of the long and short apron pieces.

With the biscuit joiner, attach the legs and apron pieces. With a table this narrow, it is usually quite easy to walk it through a doorway, although taking it apart might make for easier shipping at some unknown future time.

There's a good reason for laying out and cutting the biscuit joints while the material is still unsanded: only the rough edges face "in" towards the aprons. You can lay out the best matches for the boards before cutting and slotting. Before cutting, I mark my inside ends with an off-center square that shows where the edges should come together (Illus. 28-6).

Saw a ¼"-deep kerf 2¼" from the ends of each apron piece for the corner brackets to ride in; if there are biscuits in the corners, there's no real need to install the hanger bolts in the corners.

With the saw set at 1¾" high, set 15" stops on the mitre gauge to mark the ends of the cuts, and then saw from the center out to remove material to lower the middle section of the table. Alternatively, this could be done with a band saw, scroll saw, or even with a sabre saw. I find that the quickest, most accurate cutting is done on the table saw (Illus. 28-7); even without switching to dado blades, cutting away the middle section takes at most only five minutes.

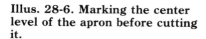

Illus. 28-6. Marking the center level of the apron before cutting it.

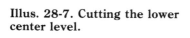

Illus. 28-7. Cutting the lower center level.

After the middle section has been removed, the table's base can be sanded and assembled. Sanding the pieces through 80 and 120 grit should take you less than 20 minutes, and it should consume about ⅓ each of the two abrasive discs. By contrast, sanding this far *after* assembly will take at least an hour, use more material, and yield less good results.

After assembling the base, test-fit the three tops, and trim and adjust them for a close fit. Some bird's-eye maple for the top may be wasted as you attempt to get the best pattern, but small scraps of this wonderful material always have a way of getting used.

Sand against sawn rather than jointed edges whenever possible; bird's-eye maple is notorious for tearing out and leaving pits when jointed. After sanding it smooth, put a ¼″ round on all edges, starting with the ends; use a clamped-on extra piece to keep the end from just tearing off the side grain; end grain is more likely to tear out, but rounding the edge grain will usually solve the problem of torn-out edges.

The lower middle piece is best left straight (unrounded) inside the table apron pieces where the maple will meet some cherry; rounding the edges would just create a dust catcher. Rout to the line, watching carefully, to avoid burning the piece.

Using a handsaw, cut 45° mitres where the high and low tops meet; then cut a 10⁵⁄₁₆″ x 1¾″ piece with mitres at each end. Install these pieces the neatest way you know how; I tacked them in place and filled the tack holes with results that are, to my way of thinking, *much less than spectacular.* If you tack the holes, be sure to predrill for the tacks and to countersink them well; this way, if all goes reasonably well, your damage will be minimal. If I had this to do over, I would screw the pieces in place, countersinking as deeply as possible and capping the screws with cherry plugs. Better yet, I might screw them and the sides with corner blocks where all the fasteners would be absolutely invisible unless one were under the table seeking them.

Before mounting the tops, finish sanding them

(Illus. 28-8). A brief consideration of the abrasives I used might convince you of the value of using power sanders. First of all, one can sand smoother with 120-grit abrasive on a sander than one can sand with 150-grit abrasive doing the work by hand. Second, a good sander will eventually pay for itself in saved abrasive; machine-sanding uses less material.

Illus. 28-8. **Sanding the tops with a belt sander. Three types of sanders—belt, random orbit, and palm—should be useful for this project. Be sure to wear hearing protection when you sand for extended periods of time.**

After sanding the tops, apply the finish of your choice to them; I treated the bird's-eye maple with a clear-varnish finish. The cherry probably looked too much like the maple for the project to be spectacular right away, so there were a couple of alternatives; one of them was to treat the table with lye (caustic soda), which causes the color to "age" much more rapidly. Because this had the drawback of raising the grain, and because I wanted results right away, I elected to use Formby's® Tung Oil Cherry Wiping Stain, which was a good match for the matching clear varnish. I used this material because it was available locally and came in very small, reasonably inexpensive containers. If you have a finish that you prefer, use it.

If you're one of those people who doesn't like to have stained furniture legs resting directly on carpeting, you may wish to add plastic or metal feet to the project; if these feet are very tall, you may want to shorten the legs appropriately.

The biscuit joiner can be used to cut several slots for the tabletop connectors; even though the table sections are small, I used four connectors for each section. It's good to have a very long

bench to stand the table on for this assembly. This is one table whose top can't be installed by laying the table top-side down because the middle section would still have to be supported somehow.

An excellent last step before putting the project in its place of honor is to give it a couple of good coats of wax. Another really good idea is to sign and date the underside of your projects so that your growth as a craftsperson will be plainly visible for anyone who knows where to look for the dates.

29.
Sofa Table with Queen Anne Legs

Sofa tables are extremely popular nowadays. The table described and illustrated here has commercial cherry Queen Anne legs purchased from The Woodworker's Store. The legs are 28″ long and provide 5½″ room for apron materials.

A template for the aprons was made of scrap plywood; it was cut outside the line, and then sanded to the line (Illus. 29-4 and 29-5). After the aprons were laid out with the template, the pieces were cut separately (Illus. 29-6 and 29-7), but

Illus. 29-1. Sofa table with Queen Anne legs. Also see page F of the color section.

Parts List for the Sofa Table with Queen Anne Legs

Label	Part	Quantity	Thickness	Width	Length
A	Top	1	¾″	15¾″	46″
B	Long Apron	2	¾″	5⅜″	36³⁄₆″
C	Short Apron	2	¾″	5⅜″	8″
D	Legs*	4			28″

*Commercial legs purchased from the Woodworker's Store.

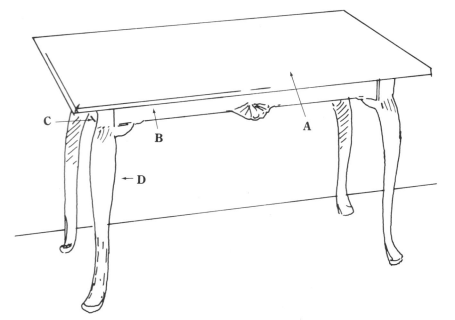

Illus. 29-2. Drawing of sofa table with Queen Anne legs.

Illus. 29-3. Cutting stock to length on the radial arm saw.

Illus. 29-4. Cutting the template for the apron pieces.

Illus. 29-5. Sanding the template for the apron pieces.

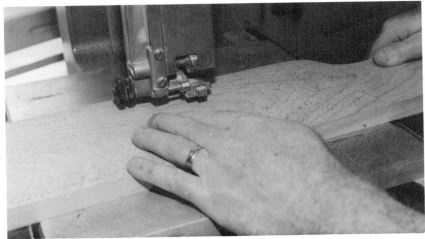

Illus. 29-6 and 29-7. Cutting the apron pieces. Note that Illus. 29-7 shows a cutoff holding the kerf open.

Illus. 29-7.

then sanded together to ensure they matched quite precisely (Illus. 29-8).

Illus. 29-8. Sanding the long aprons while they are clamped together.

The shell pattern was drawn with French curves and then carved (Illus. 29-9) with a V-tool and #3 and #5 gouges (these were Pfeil "Swiss made" gouges, so you may have to use a different number if you elect to carve the shell; the project would likely be just as handsome without the shell).

The maker screwed the table together with Sheetrock screws after drilling holes for them with a pocket-hole drill bit, eschewing the jig that usually accompanies such bits (Illus. 29-10–29-13). He began each hole by drilling straight in to start the cut, and then angling quickly. The cuts

were started ¾" or so from the ends of the apron pieces and continued into the legs. Drill the pilot holes with their countersunk areas first, and then attach the screws. Be sure to screw the short aprons on first; the long aprons (Illus. 29-14) will permit the screw gun to be operated from inside the small frame, but the short aprons would be difficult to attach with *any* fastening method if they were attached second.

After the base was made, we worked on the

Illus. 29-9. Carving the shell.

Illus. 29-10. Laying out for pocket-hole drilling.

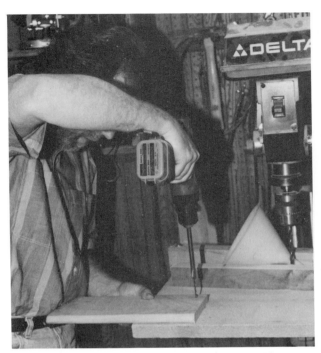

Illus. 29-11. Start with the drill at about 90°.

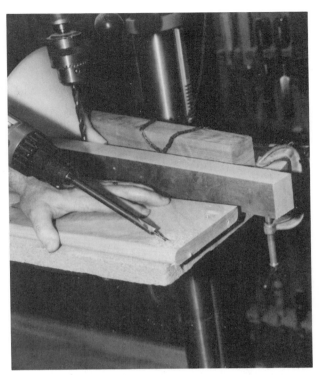

Illus. 29-13. Test cuts are a good idea when planning freehand drilling like this.

Illus. 29-12. Then lower the angle and proceed with the cut.

Illus. 29-14. Screwing the long apron to the legs.

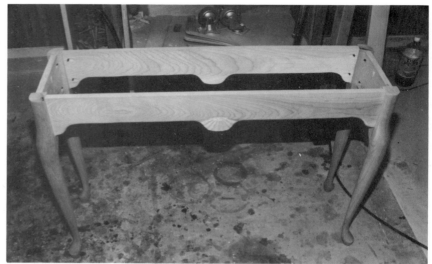

Illus. 29-15. The completed leg set.

top (29-16). We rounded the top of the tabletop with a CMT #856–601 bit, and then used a CMT #838–704 bit for the underside. It's really handy to have two routers so you can use the same setup on each edge as you go around the material (Illus. 29-17–29-19). Be sure to rout the end grain first, and to securely clamp some extra boards on to protect the piece against tear-out; this is particularly important when routing with large bits. The resulting profile is terrific!

The top was fastened to the base with one

screw through each of the short aprons (Illus. 29-20 and 29-21).

Hoping to give the wood a more "aged" appearance, the maker used a cherry penetrating stain on this cherry (Illus. 29-22) with, at best, mixed success; it took a great deal of extra effort to come up with the satisfactory results that he finally got. While there are as many successful finishing methods as there are woodworkers, Chapter 9 describes finishes that are easy enough to use that they will work for virtually everyone.

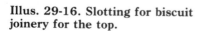

Illus. 29-16. Slotting for biscuit joinery for the top.

Illus. 29-17. Two routers with the bits used to cut the moulding profile on the edges of the top.

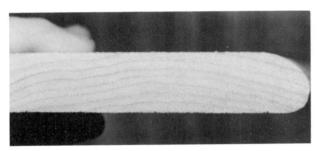

Illus. 29-18. This profile was created with CMT # 856-601 and 838-704 bits.

Illus. 29-19. The CMT # 856-601 bit.

Illus. 29-20. Fastening the top to the leg set through a pair of pocket holes.

Illus. 29-21. The top on the completed leg set.

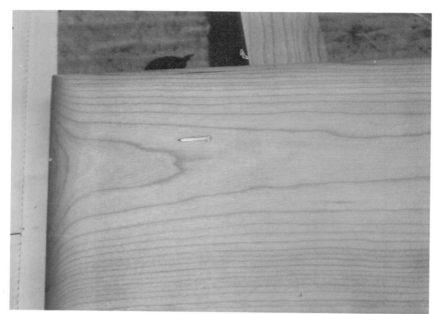

Illus. 29-22. The maker's trade-mark, half a brass tack glued and sanded flush.

Illus. 29-23. Adding a stain to the project.

30.
Table with Commercial Ball-and-Claw Legs

Adams Wood Products of Morristown, Tennessee, has a catalogue which shows legs and other parts so intriguing that I ordered a set of ball-and-claw legs for a table (Illus. 30-1–30-5). To be sure, these legs are expensive, almost as expensive as legs I've seen in stores—but there's a difference: These are better matched.

The ball-and-claw legs I ordered had enough rail to make joining them with a biscuit joiner possible. When the legs cost upwards of $20 *each*, there's no room for error in assembling the table.

I feel far more confident with a stack of biscuits than with a row of dowels; after all, biscuiting the apron pieces to the legs is very easy.

Of course, I could have made the legs with a band saw and a set of files, but these legs actually match—and I doubt that, at my current shop rate, I could have reproduced them for what I paid for them ready-made.

Since the joinable portion of each leg is only 4″, the biscuit joiner's face is wider than the work, so layout of the joints is somewhat different (Illus.

Illus. 30-1. Table with ball-and-claw legs.

Parts List for Table with Commercial Ball-and-Claw Legs

Label	Part	Quantity	Thickness	Width	Length
A	Leg	4			
B	Short Apron	2	³⁄₄″	4″	20″
C	Long Apron	2	³⁄₄″	4″	24″
D	Built-Up Top	1	1″	1″	30″

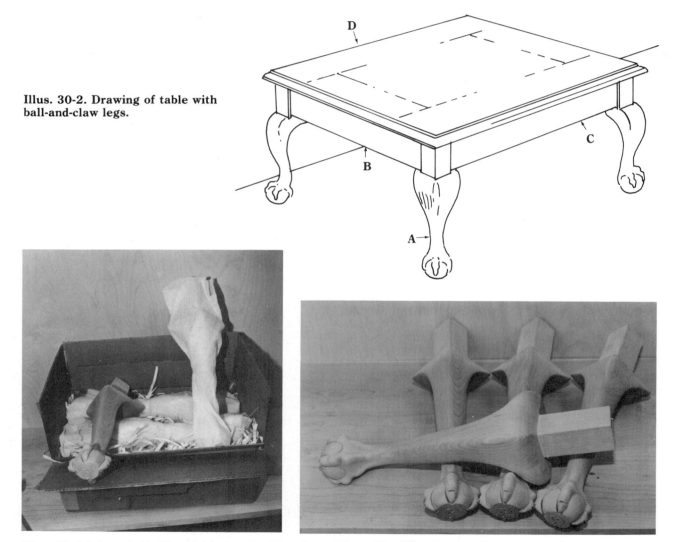

Illus. 30-2. Drawing of table with ball-and-claw legs.

Illus. 30-3 (above left). The nicely detailed legs from Adams Wood Products arrive well-packed. Illus. 30-4 (above right). A view of a nicely matched leg set.

Illus. 30-5. This side view shows the "ears," which are the upper parts of the legs.

Illus. 30-6. The joiner overlaps the face to be joined.

30-6–30-8). There is no room to center the joints. First, I marked each side of a leg at the machine's centerpoint; then I transferred those marks to the apron pieces. After that bit of layout is done, connecting the leg and apron pieces goes very smoothly.

Using a biscuit joiner set for size #0 biscuits, I added a few slots for the tabletop connectors that will join the top. Then I glued up a 26″ x 30″ top, as near a full inch thick as possible. After cleaning up the assembly and putting a decorative edge on it, I put some finish on it.

Illus. 30-7. Mark the face.

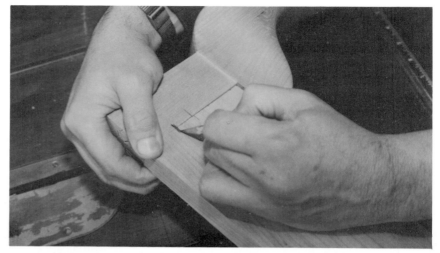

Illus. 30-8. Then transfer the marks to the apron pieces.

Illus. 30-9. After the insert has been placed in the top, hand-plane it until it has a flat surface. Here I'm using a Record No. 3c plane, which has a corrugated bottom.

Illus. 30-10. This project is good-looking, even when it is still in the clamps.

31.
Cigarette/Lamp Table

This graceful little table has been popular for well over 100 years. I have seen two different versions of this table. The first was a model dating from the early years of the 20th century that I inherited from my grandmother. I've seen "Shaker" versions of this table in cherry as well.

The square top of this table overhangs the legs and apron by 2″ all around; the aprons are very wide; indeed, in the bird's-eye maple specimen shown in this chapter, the apron pieces are wider than they are long. The legs have been made from 1⅝″ stock which has been tapered to about ⅝″. One of the main advantages of making this chair-side table rather than buying it is that you can custom-select the table's height to match the height of the armchair alongside it.

Making this table is very easy. Cut your stock to the proper thickness and then cut the pieces to length and width per the cutting list. Taper the legs at 8″ from the top from their full 1⅝″ to about ⅝″ (Illus. 31-3 and 31-4). Sand the saw marks out of all eight taper cuts before assembly. Saw kerfs for the table attachers to ride in ½″ from the top edge of the pieces. If you want rounded-over rather than just broken edges, take the apron pieces to your router table before assembly. Then sand all leg and apron pieces prior to assembly.

Mock up the assembly on your workbench, and lay out the best locations for the biscuit joints (Illus. 31-5 and 31-6). I used two biscuits per joint, 2″ and 5″ from the top of the apron; these two

biscuits are more than enough to hold the assembly together, even though I glued *only* the biscuit slots because it would be useless to try to glue end grain to face grain. Join the aprons to the legs

Illus. 31-1. Cigarette/lamp table. Also see page A of the color section.

195

Parts List for the Cigarette/Lamp Table

Label	Part	Quantity	Thickness	Width	Length
A	Square Top	1	¾″	12″–13″	12″–13″
B	Leg	4	1⅝″	1⅝″	24⅜″
C	Apron	4	¾″	7¾″	7¼″

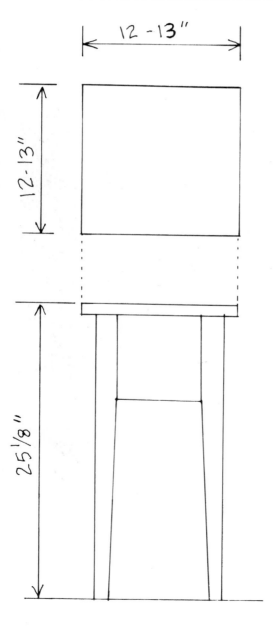

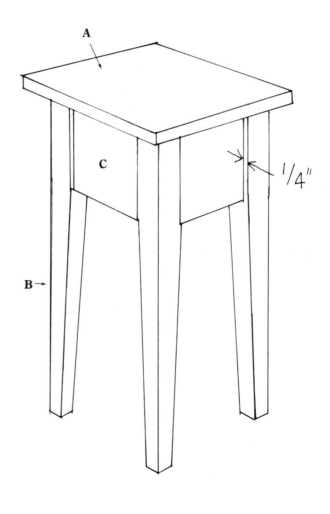

Illus. 31-2. Top, side, and full views of cigarette/lamp table.

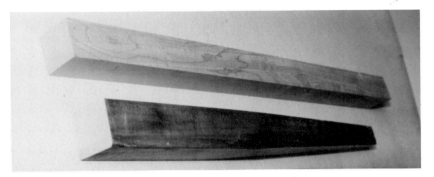

Illus. 31-3. The legs for this table must be tapered enough to be graceful. The lower piece isn't sufficiently tapered, so it looks "clunkier" than the straight piece above it. Part of this table was made from recycled wood.

Illus. 31-4. The taper jig is set up to reduce the 1¾″ stock to about ⅝″ at the bottom. This is a much more acceptable taper than shown in Illus. 31-3.

Illus. 31-6.

Illus. 31-5 and 31-6. Lay out your pieces carefully, so that face-grain legs align with face-grain legs, etc. Illus. 31-6 shows a principal failure of this table: after the final gluing, I stood the table up and set the top on it, only to discover that on a couple of sides of the legs the face and edge grain is mixed. Plan for grain-matching even before taper-cutting.

with a pair of biscuits, for best results (Illus. 31-7). After the glue has dried, biscuit the two pairs together.

After the glue has dried, sand the leg assembly through 150 or 220 grit. Attach the top using either shop-made fasteners or commercial fasteners, which allow for expansion.

One last fine sanding should precede the application of finish. While I believe that a clear finish is always the best choice, many people are sure to prefer that the maple be finished with some amber additive in the varnish so it looks the way clear-finished maple has looked until recent years. Some others may find the "white" look of the Hydrocote-finished maple to be an attractive novelty.

It may be worth noting that I made this table and applied the first coat of finish in *part* of a single afternoon. Working with very fancy maple, my cost for the table was about $20, inclusive of ab-

rasives and finishing materials. Part of the reason for this is that we've bought the finishes and abrasives in bulk and are "paying" only for what we use. If you're starting from scratch, you might spend as much as double what I did to build a comparable table, but you will have abrasives and finish on hand for your next project.

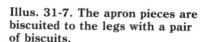

Illus. 31-7. The apron pieces are biscuited to the legs with a pair of biscuits.

32.
A Table with Inset Tops

The inset tops used on this simple table (Illus. 32-1 and 32-2) can be made of different varieties of wood and other material, and can be of different sizes. This design started with a need for a low table to position between a pair of low but comfortable rattan chairs in my own living room. I began with my favorite wood, cherry, but the table would be inexpensive to make, almost regardless of material.

Begin the project by cutting all the pieces to size. I used a small-radius round-over bit on all four corners of the legs and on both sides of the bottoms of the apron. Be sure to cut the slot ½"

from the top of the apron for the tabletop fasteners to ride in.

Join each apron piece to each leg with a stacked row of biscuits; position two biscuits about ¼" from both the inside and outside edge of each apron piece's end. After brief clamping, scrape away any glue squeeze-out and sand the base through 150 grit. Attach furniture feet if you're inclined to use them.

When I made this table, I mitred the top pieces after cutting a ½" by ½" rabbet off the inside of each piece. If I were to build this project again, I'd be inclined to butt the joints, perhaps biscuiting

Illus. 32-1. Table with inset tops. Also see page B of the color section.

Parts List for Table with Inset Tops

Label	Part	Quantity	Thickness	Width	Length
A	Leg	4	1¾″	1¾″	15¼″
B	Short Apron	2	¾″	3″	10¼″
C	Long Apron	2	¾″	3″	12¾″
D	Short Top	2	¾″	3¼″	14¾″
E	Long Top	2	¾″	3¼″	19″
F	Inset		at least ½″	9″	13½″

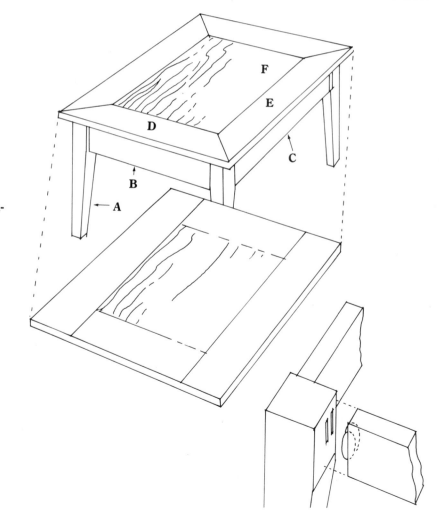

Illus. 32-2. Drawing of table with inset tops.

them as I biscuited the apron pieces to the legs. Then I would cut a rabbet on the inside with a bit like the CMT 800–508 bit, squaring the corners with a chisel. Mitre joints are neat and effective, but this seems to be a location where a butt joint might work better.

After the tabletop has been assembled and mounted to the base, all that remains is to cut the inserts to fit. This table has a beautiful piece of bird's-eye maple (Illus. 32-3), a piece of grey granite Corian® (Illus. 32-4), a piece of spalted maple (page B of color section), and is bordered at either end with a piece of old rosewood veneer. Had I been less than pleased with these inserts, I'd have added cherry, walnut, a couple of highly figured veneers (like olive-ash burl), smoked glass, or tile, to name but a few other options. Some of these options will be treated more thoroughly in the following chapters.

The insets all have a rabbet, so that ½" x ½"

Illus. 32-4. A Corian® inset top.

Illus. 32-3. An inset of bird's-eye maple. An inset of this kind was used on the table illustrated in this chapter.

is the thickness of the top edge. If you're planning to use smoked glass, you might want to make the rabbet somewhat "thinner"; otherwise, you'll end up shimming the material.

The Corian here is cut to be higher than the wood surface. I rounded over the edges of one face, and let the material ride about ¼" above the rest of the tabletop; I could just as well have cut a rabbet and let it ride flush in my inset. While the material can be cut nicely with sharp carbide-tipped cutters, the dust this material generates is more dangerous to equipment and people than is normal wood sawdust, so use as much dust-control equipment as you have available, wear your eye shields *and* your respiratory protection while working this material, and clean the chips frequently. While Corian is costly to buy in sheets, averaging about $25 per square foot, building contractors will often sell you "sink holes" and other odd pieces for a fraction of the cost; unless you need a really huge piece, this is the way to buy it!

33.
Building a Table in Two Hours

One day my wife and I looked at tables in the furniture department of an upscale "discount" department store. The least-expensive table in the place was "on sale" for $129.99. It was called a "lamp table" and was offered in a choice of maple or oak. It consisted of four legs with no taper to them, four pieces of apron, and a glued-up hardwood top. Its edges were not rounded over or even "softened" very much.

I came home and made the table shown in this chapter (Illus. 33-1–33-4) in approximately two hours. And though normally the cost of the project should not be a top priority for the hobbyist woodworker, it should be noted that building this project will save a great deal of money.

Here's the procedure for making the table in approximately two hours. First, select, plane, and cut to size pieces from stock on hand (Illus. 33-

Illus. 33-1. Wide view of the table.

Illus. 33-2. End view of the table.

Parts List for a Two-Hour Table

Label	Part	Quantity	Thickness	Width	Length
A	Leg	4	1¾″	1¾″	24″
B	Long Apron	2	¾″	3½″	22″
C	Short Apron	2	¾″	3½″	12″
D	Top	1	¾″	17″	28″
	Biscuits	8			
	Corner Irons	4			
	Hanger Bolts	4			
	Wing Nuts with Washers	4			

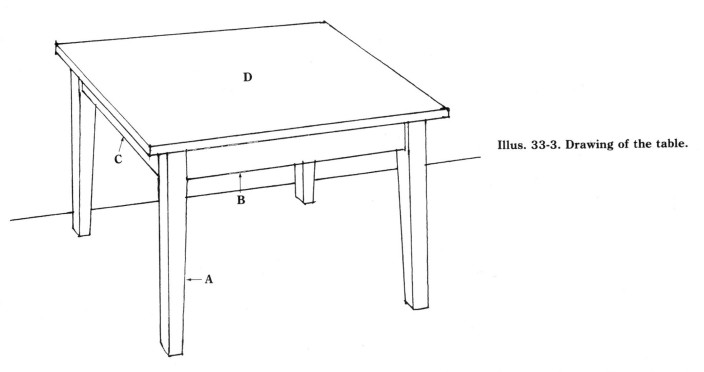

Illus. 33-3. Drawing of the table.

4). Then glue up the top using half a dozen biscuits for levelling. It may be worth noting that if you don't have a shop full of tools, you may be able to buy glued-up stock pretty close to these sizes at a well-stocked building center.

Cut the tapers on the legs. Lay these out by

Illus. 33-4. Cutting out the center of the front and back aprons.

Illus. 33-5. Rounding over the leg edges.

Illus. 33-6. A look at the underside of the table. Note how the wing nut on the hanger bolt makes the table quite portable.

eye with a standard taper jig. Next, sand these legs smooth and mount the hanger bolts 1¾" from the tops on the inside corners.

Next, cut the saw kerfs 2⅝" from the inside ends and ½" from the inside tops of the apron pieces. Round over the bottoms of the apron pieces, inside and out; round over the legs on all four long edges (Illus. 33-5), and round over the top on all exposed edges. You'll make best time at this by using a router table.

Then mount the table legs to the apron pieces using Woodcraft supply corners (Illus. 33-7) or other corner irons. Using a Vix-Bit® to drill the holes and a power driver to mount the corner irons saves a good bit of time. Use these tools again as you mount the base to the top; I used two table irons on each side and one on each end.

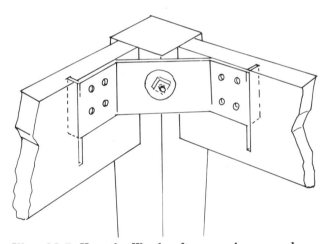

Illus. 33-7. How the Woodcraft corner brace works.

I spent 20 minutes sanding the table. I began with a belt sander, keeping it moving every second it was in contact with the wood. Then I advanced to a random orbital sander with the same grit as the belt sander; if you belt-sand at 80-grit, that's the grit to start with. I advanced through a careful sanding at 120 grit, and then quickly sanded it with 150-grit sandpaper. Then I advanced to my pad sander using 150-grit, and then 180-grit sandpaper. Keep each of these sanding machines moving when they are in contact with the project; it's not necessary to bear down hard with any of them.

Finally, I sanded over the table quickly with 220-grit sandpaper. Anytime the table's top was on the bench "top"-side down, I used a router pad to keep the top from being damaged by the fine dust and grit on the bench (Illus. 33-8 and 33-9). As I advanced to finishing, I exchanged the router pad for an old bath towel (Illus. 33-10); this kept

Illus. 33-8. Use a sanding or router pad to protect assembly during sanding.

Illus. 33-9. Note that the PSA (pressure-sensitive adhesive) permits you to use sandpaper longer than might be expected when using a clamped-in abrasive. These PSA abrasives are well worth the slight difference in cost.

the top on something soft without risking damage to its smooth surface.

My first step in finishing was to blow all the dust off the project with compressed air. Then I

Illus. 33-10. Put a towel or other soft fabric under the table when you work on it on the bench. This keeps the top on something soft without risking damage to its smooth surface.

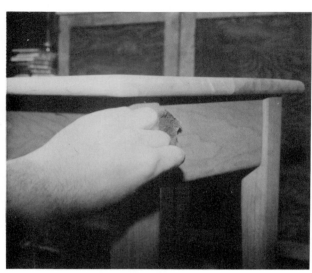

Illus. 33-11. Applying the finish.

applied three coats of Hydrocote polyurethane (Illus. 33-11); three coats at roughly ten minutes per coat takes 30 minutes. I applied the material with a damp rag; if you do likewise, wearing rubber gloves is imperative; otherwise, the material will stick to your skin. I quickly sanded the table with 440- or 600-grit sandpaper and wiped it with a damp rag between coats. Finally, I spent another ten minutes waxing the piece.

All in all, I spent slightly over two enjoyable hours building this project. Remember, however, woodworking as a hobby isn't really about time and money. What it *is* about is stress reduction and the joy of accomplishment at a job that we can see is very well done.

34.
Large Coffee Tables

Illus. 34-1–31-4 show two versions of very old tables that appear to be coming back into style. They are large and heavy. The tables date into the last century. They are made of oak, often nailed together.

The apron pieces are 6⅛″ wide; two are 57¼″ long, and the others are 27½″ long. The legs are 2¾″ square, 19⅝″ long, and turned. The top is 30″ wide and 60″ long. It is more than 1″ thick and has a drip groove (Illus. 34-6). The total height is 21″. The tiny drawers seem almost useless. The oak top on one table has split from end to end, yet the table remains beautiful.

Modern construction would make biscuiting the aprons to the legs perfectly acceptable, but if you are trying to make the piece according to methods of the periods in which it was originally made, you'll want to add about 1¼″ to 1½″ to each end for tenons. These tenons can be simply glued into mortises on the legs, or they can be glued and pegged.

Illus. 34-1 (above left). A wide view of the coffee table as it's used every day. Illus. 34-2 (above right). An end view of the coffee table.

Illus. 34-3 and 34-4. Views of a much abused table similar to the table shown in Illus. 34-1 and 34-2.

Illus. 34-4.

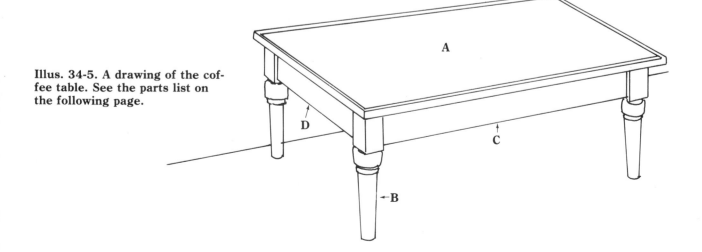

Illus. 34-5. A drawing of the coffee table. See the parts list on the following page.

Parts List for Large Coffee Table

Label	Part	Quantity	Thickness	Width	Length
A	Top	1	1⅛″	30″	60″
B	Leg	4	2¾″	2¾″	19⅝″
C	Long Apron	2	1″	6⅛″	51¾″
D	Short Apron	2	1″	6⅛″	21¾″

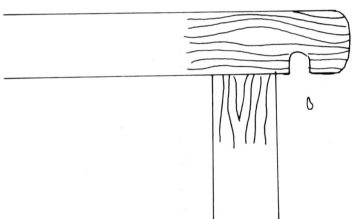

Illus. 34-6. A drip groove keeps liquids from running down the sides of the furniture.

35.
Cocktail Table with a Pair of End Tables

Honduras mahogany is the ideal material for making a cocktail table because the top can be made of a single, very handsome wide plank. The simple elegance of this piece is such that it would look good no matter what material you used. The design permits modifications to suit your particular needs. It can be made longer/shorter, wider/narrower, and/or taller/lower with very little trouble.

When I made the prototype shown in Illus. 35-1 and 35-2, I had just acquired an antique beading plane, so the table has more beading than a table of this size really needs. In hindsight I wonder why I didn't instead try carving something on the rails. Simple and handsome designs could be carved even by untutored novices, and mahogany carves so beautifully.

When you buy the wide mahogany plank, it would probably be wise to have it surfaced by your lumber merchant; his planer is wide enough, and yours almost certainly is *not*. My piece of 1¼″-thick mahogany nearly 20″ wide was so flat that it surfaced beautifully to nearly 1¼″ thick. When I got the plank home, I cut it to length and marked the tapers on each side. I cut them on the band saw; though, if I had to do it over again, I'd have used just a hand-held sabre saw. I smoothed and refined these tapers with a block plane and a spokeshave.

After determining which side of the top was the "top" surface, I lay it on the bench "top" down and proceeded to relieve the sides away from the edges for about 3″, using a drawknife, a block

Illus. 35-1. The cocktail table.

Illus. 35-2. The end table with its drawer open.

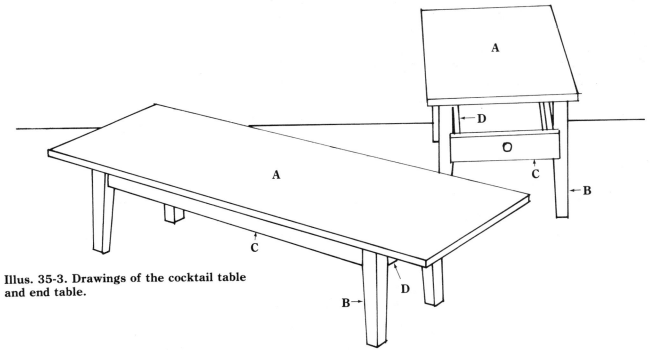

Illus. 35-3. Drawings of the cocktail table and end table.

Parts List for an End Table

Label	Part	Quantity	Thickness	Width	Length
A	Top	1	1″	20″	28″
B	Leg	4	2″	2″	19½″ (adjust to needs)
C	Drawer Front	1	1″	3½″	13⅜″
D	Drawer Side	2	½″	2¼″	20″
	Side Apron	2	1″	3″	24″
	Rear Apron	1	1″	3″	14½″
	Side Apron Filler	2		2¼″	Cut to Length Needed
	Drawer Support	2	½″	2″	Cut to Length Needed
	Drawer Back	1	½″	2″	13¼″
	Front Support Rail	1	½″	1½″	14½″
	Feet (⅞ in Diameter)	4			

Parts List for the Cocktail Table

Label	Part	Quantity	Thickness	Width	Length
A	Top	1	1¼″	18″	52″
B	Legs	4	2″	2″	13⅜″
C	Side Rail	2	¾″	2¾″	40¼″
D	End Rail	2	¾″	2¾″	12¾″
	Corner Brace	4	1⅝″	1⅝″	6″
	Fastening Board	2	¾″	2″	38¼″
	Furniture Feet	4			
	Fasteners (FHWS # 10 x 1½″)	16			

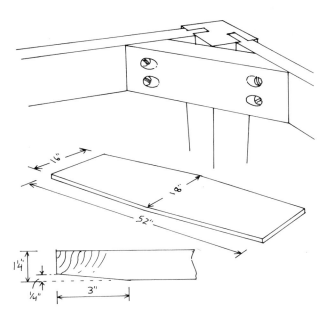

Illus. 35-5. Details of the cocktail table.

plane, and a spokeshave. When I felt this relief made the piece look markedly lighter, I turned the top over and used a cabinet scraper to remove the milling marks from the visible surface. It may be worth noting here that no sandpaper ever touched this project. Whether it was worth the extra time to scrape the wood smooth rather than just use a belt sander is a moot point, but if you have more time than money, you may find scraping to be a good idea.

The final step of this top preparation was to scrub it mightily with its own shavings, burnishing it until it literally shone.

Before I started making the base, I began a finishing schedule consisting of first an application of Watco Medium-Walnut Oil, followed by at least half a dozen coats of Watco Natural Oil, and, finally, a good waxing. The reason for starting this now is that the top needs a greater buildup of finishing material than does the base.

Making the base is very straightforward. Square up four pieces of 2″ x 2″ stock 13⅜″ long. Once this is done, mark and cut mortises for the side and end rails. After marking the legs for mortises, cut the mortises with a router. Once the

mortises are cut, mark the tapers on the legs, and set your taper jig to cut them on the table saw. If you do not have a taper jig, this is the perfect time to make one. My taper jig is simply a pair of 1″ x 2″ x 19″ boards that are hinged at one end and have a stop block at the other end. On the end with the stop block, I screwed a piece of ¼″ x 1″ x 4″ plywood with a ¼″ channel routed through about 2½″ of it, to permit the stop block to be adjusted with a wing nut.

Cut the tapers by giving each piece two passes through the saw, one pass on each mortised face. Clean up these saw cuts with a plane or spokeshave, and scrape them clean. Or, you may simply sand them smooth.

Rip your rails to a width of 2¾″ and cut them to length. My side rails are 38¼″ plus 1″ on either end for tenons. The end rails are 10¾″ plus 1″ on either end for tenons. I cut the tenons on the table saw by setting a stop block to make the cuts 1″ from the ends; be sure to set the stop blocks relative to the inside rather than the outside of the saw blade. You can cut the tenon by repeatedly passing over the blade or by turning the piece on its end and ripping off thin slices; the second method makes better-looking tenons, but it doesn't really save time unless you are doing production work, and the slightly "ruffled" effect made by repeated passes over the blade probably leaves a better gluing surface and is definitely safer.

After the tenons are cut, make a test fitting. Make any needed adjustments for a perfect fit. Then smooth and/or decorate these rails before gluing the legs and rails together. Before gluing, cut a ⅜″ deep by ¼″ wide dado ½″ from the top of the long rails. Glue and clamp the legs and rails. A framing clamp will prove helpful.

When the glue has set, scrape away any "bubles" and burnish the base before fastening the top to it. Cut a rabbet in the two remaining pieces so that they will fit into the dado cut in the long rails, flush to the top. With these inserts positioned but not glued or otherwise fastened in place, put the base onto the underside of the top, positioning it carefully, and apply three well-spaced screws (I used #8 x 1¼″ screws) through the insert into the top. This will hold the top on nicely and still allow the wood to move.

Disassemble the table and apply the base's coat of Watco Medium-Walnut Oil. Reassemble it and apply a couple of coats of Watco Natural Oil to the entire table. The single application of the dark Watco Oil simply helps to hasten the appearance of the mahogany which results from its tendency to oxidize. If you skip the dark coat, the table will darken naturally, for mahogany starts out looking rather like a new penny, and, with time, will become richer in color. After your table has been waxed, it is ready to be put to use.

End Tables

Like the coffee table, the tops of these end tables are crafted of a single wide plank of Honduras mahogany. The height of these tables is 20½″, but the correct height for *your* end tables should be *the height of your sofa's arm rests*. While I assume that you will build these as a matching pair, this section and the parts contain information for making a single table.

If you don't have access to a wide plank, or if you want to make the table of something other than Honduras mahogany, you will have to glue up planks to get your top. Cut and plane the plank that will be your top to 1″ x 20″ x 28″. You may want to start your finishing schedule for the top at this time, since the top will need more applications of finish than will the rest of the project.

Cut four 2″ x 2″ x 19½″ legs. Use your taper jig to taper two sides of each leg to 1″ x 1″, leaving at least 4″ of straight 2″ square at the other ends. Plane, scrape, or sand the legs free of any milling marks and proceed to mark the tapered sides of the legs for their mortises. On the pieces that you have selected to be the rear legs, cut mortises suitable for mounting 3″ stock across the back and towards each front. Cut the corresponding mor-

tises on the front legs; then, between the front legs cut a mortise for mounting a ½″ x 1½″ strip across (that is, perpendicular to) the grain, 3″ from the top of each leg. Using your table saw, two hollow-ground blades, and an appropriate tenon-cutting spacer, cut the tenons on your 1″ x 3″ x 24″ side aprons, your 1″ x 3″ x 14½″ rear apron, and your ½″ x 1½″ x 14½″ front support rail. Trial-fit, adjust, and then glue your base together, working carefully so that you don't wind up with a gluey mess.

After you have taken the base out of the clamps and cleaned up any excess glue, measure its inside sides and plane a filler strip that is thick enough to make the side rails even with the legs on the insides. Glue and screw a strip to the "bottom" of each of these "filler" inserts so that when the inserts are glued and screwed to the inside of the side aprons, they will be even with the front low railing to support the drawer. As soon as these pieces have been attached, apply feet to your project, unless, of course, you have decided not to use them.

The next step is to make a drawer. The drawer front should be 1″ x 3½″ x 13⅜″. The sides are ½″ x 2¼″ x 20″ and are dovetailed to the front and to the back, which is ½″ x 2″ x 13¼″. Before cutting the dovetails, cut a ¼″ dado 2″ from the top of the drawer front, and a ¼″ rabbet from the bottoms of each side; the drawer bottom will be screwed into this and into the back of the drawer, which will simply rest on the top of the plywood or Masonite® drawer bottom.

After all the drawer parts are dry-fitted, glue them together. This is the last step in the assembly. Sand or scrape the entire unit again, and finish per the instructions provided with the other unit, or follow your own finishing schedule. After a final waxing, the unit is ready to be put to use with the coffee table. This trio would be a handsome addition to nearly any living room or den.

36.
Pine Burl Table

*A Burl is a swirling frozen pot of marbleized color, texture
and structure; creating patterns too complex to understand
or predict. It is one of nature's amazing mysteries—the
starry galaxy within is greater than the form containing it.* *

Thus Mark Lindquist described a burl nearly a decade ago. The swirls and figures resulting from end-grain budding are so beautiful and peculiar to each burl that these patterns cry out to be displayed.

In early July, 1987, a huge tree on the north shore of Lake Bemidji, Minnesota, was blown over by a storm. Contemplating the burl that grew on that tree led Dr. H. B. Roholt to build a trio of pine burl tables. They aren't something that you'll likely be able to copy directly, but rather something that may inspire you to make similar projects of your own. It's a project that involves far more waiting time than actual building time, so it's safe to say this might be a project best tackled by the patient woodworker.

By mid-August, 1987, a 3½ x 4 *foot* burl on the tree trunk was sliced and chain-sawed into nine 4″-thick slices; Illus. 36-4 shows a hired lumberjack making the cuts. It's usually wise to hire someone to tackle jobs that are too big, rough, or dangerous, or are far beyond your level of expertise. Initial preparation of all nine slabs involved removal of bark and of underlying detritus and insects from all slab edges and from the areas where bark inclusions had occurred on the slab surfaces. This is tedious work even with the use of various chipping, pounding, and prying tools.

Realizing that the relative structural stability of the slabs could be achieved only by drying the

slabs enough so that moisture content would equilibrate with in-house environmental conditions, and suspecting that a very slow and gradual drying would result in less burl splitting, drying, and

Illus. 36-1. Table I. (The photos in this chapter courtesy of Dr. H. B. Roholt.)

*Mark Lindquist, "Harvesting Burls," *Fine Woodworking*, July/August, 1984, pp. 67–71.

Illus. 36-2. Table II.

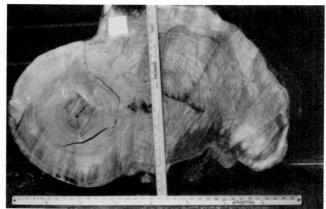

Illus. 36-3. A close-up of a burl.

cracking, Dr. Roholt chose air- rather than kiln-drying. A sealant (urethane varnish or paraffin wax) to slow the drying rates was applied to the slab surfaces, but not to the edges. Orthorix antifungal spray was then applied to all edges to prevent or retard mould growth while the slabs were in storage.

Dr. Roholt achieved the equivalent of initial slow outside-air-drying by placing all slabs in his unheated but ventilated garage attic. All slabs were periodically weighed, and by September, 1988, slab weights were stable with weight losses in the range of 25 percent and with metre-measured moisture contents of 14–16 percent.

Illus. 36-4. Here a lumberjack is sawing out a large log.

The three slabs selected for tables were then transferred to in-house conditions in an unused bedroom. Three months later their weights were again stable with total weight losses in the range

Drying Times of Burls

Date	Slab 1 — Weight (Pounds)	Slab 2 — Weight (Pounds)	Slab 3 — Weight (Pounds)
September, 1987	44¼	67¾	68¾
November, 1987	38½	64	
January, 1988	31¾	60¼	
February, 1988	32⅛	51½	
March, 1988	32¼	51¼	
January, 1989	29¼	48½	44¼

of 28–35 percent and with metre-measured moisture contents of 8–9 percent. Since they had lost about one-third of their weight, they were brought into the shop. If you're going to air-dry material like this, check the material fairly often, but still wait for the drying material to lose about one-third of its weight. Then check the moisture content with an appropriate moisture metre.

The chart above contains information on the drying times of these slabs. As you study these weights, be aware that the burls are white pine and that the tree was felled in early July, 1987 and sliced on August 14, 1987.

In the fall of 1989, the processing of the three tabletops began. Here is a description of the tabletops used on the three tables. The top for the first table is an eccentric oval. It is 2″ x 11½″ x 13″. It is 22¾″ high and weighs 14 pounds. The top for the second table is an irregular oval. It is 2¾″ x 25″ x 34″, and is 18½″ high and weighs 56 pounds. The top for the third table is an irregular oval. Its dimensions are 3½″ x 20″ x 29½″, it is 19″ high, and it weighs 47 pounds.

The top surface of each slab was levelled with a hand power planer (Illus. 36-5) and with progressively finer belt-, orbital-, and hand-sanding (Illus. 36-6). Uniform slab thickness was obtained by first cutting a ¼″ wide x ½″ deep marking dado

Illus. 36-5. Burl with planer.

around the slab with a dado head horizontally positioned in a radial arm saw. This was done by placing the previously levelled top surface of the slab downward on the radial arm saw table and then slowly rotating the slab edge into the running dado head (Illus. 36-7). A chain saw was then used to remove the excess with the dado serving as a guide to the chain-saw cut (Illus. 36-8). The new underside of each slab, now parallel with the top, was then power-planed and rough-sanded.

When needed, the slab edges were trimmed with a band saw, with each slab placed on a previously made large table extension. The edges were then flap-sanded. The slab used for tables II and III consisted of burls and an attached adjacent

Illus. 36-6. Dr. Roholt sanding with the belt sander.

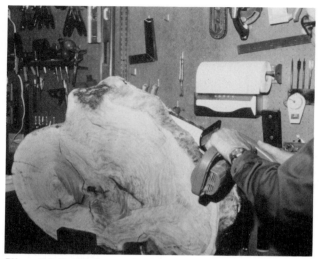

Illus. 36-8. Chain-sawing the bottom parallel to the top. Using the notches made at the radial arm saw is one of the quicker, more efficient ways of making the bottoms even.

Illus. 36-7. Evenly notching the edge with the radial arm saw.

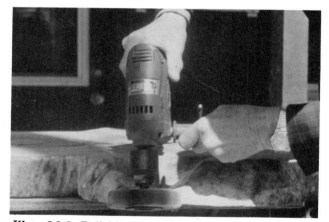

Illus. 36-9. Polishing the edges.

tree trunk. Just burls with appropriate edge-trimming were used for table I.

Surface and edge cracks and voids which might have detracted from table function or appearance were converted to areas of interest when Dr. Roholt filled them with a tinted two-part polymer. In this case, Envirotex and Chemco Transparent Resin dyes (Environmental Technology, Inc., P.O Box 365, Fields Landing, California 95531) were used. To prevent the liquid polymer from bleeding into wood fibres adjacent to the filled areas, two

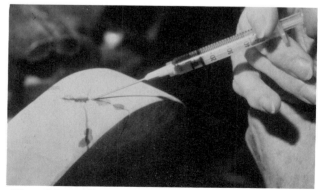

Illus. 36-10. Repairing the edge of the burr.

coats of Waterlox Transparent resin (available from Waterlox Chemical and Coatings Corporation, 9808 Meech Avenue, Cleveland, Ohio 41405) were first applied to areas receiving the polymer. To prevent leakage loss of the poured mixture while in liquid form, Dr. Roholt found that only an epoxy putty applied carefully to edge and underside surface areas of stress cracks could achieve an effective seal. The Envirotex reactive polymer shrinks very little and tends to trap very few bubbles, but it takes three days to cure to full strength. Some refilling of stress crack areas and voids had to be done to achieve a polymer surface level with the top.

After the cracks and voids were completely filled, the edges and top surfaces were sanded with progressively finer grits of sandpaper. Firm rubbing with acetone-soaked cotton-tipped swabs removed the fine sanding-induced scratches from the Envirotex.

Dr. Roholt elected not to use the two-part polymer as the "finish" for the tabletops as is often done, for he felt that this type of finish creates a tactile barrier between the wood and the table user. Polyurethane varnish cannot be used, as this would adversely react with the areas filled with polymer. A tung-oil-based varnish was selected for finishing. Tung oil has far less tendency to darken and has far more water and alcohol resistance than a linseed-oil-based finish. The Waterlox® Transparent tung-oil varnish was applied four times with a fine sanding between coats and a final 400-grit sanding.

In April, 1990, pedestal bases were made. The elm segments for Table I, which were previously soaked in PEG and then dried, were turned on Dr. Roholt's lathe. The elm segments for Tables II and III, also soaked in PEG and then dried, were turned by professional turner Jim Gabraelson on his heavier lathe. PEG is polyethylene glycol, which displaces the water in green wood to pre-vent cracking and checking as the wood dries. It stabilizes green wood enough so that you can use it quickly after processing without fear of subsequent distortion with conventional drying. However, the PEG processing makes it difficult to match a finish to untreated wood.

The pedestals were sanded. Minwax dark-walnut stain was applied to the pedestal of Table I. Honeytone amber maple aniline dye was applied to the pedestals for Tables II and III. Three coats of Waterlox Transparent were applied with between-coat sanding to all pedestals.

Circular bases for the pedestals were band-saw-cut from edge-jointed, air-dried elm, and then were rounded with a router. Three threaded brass inserts (#20 x ¼") were placed in the lower surface of each base for furniture levelers.

Dr. Roholt elected to finish the circular pedestal bottoms with an oil-based primer and two coats of an oil-based satin-black enamel because he was unable to match the finishes on the PEG-treated pedestals.

The bases were attached to the pedestal bottoms with #10 x 1½" recessed flathead screws. Medium-density-fibreboard (MDF) circles were screwed to the pedestal tops and then screwed to the underside of the tabletops with #10 x 1¾" screws. All table parts are thus separable, for ease in packing and shipping.

With the tables so finished, the grain structure is not only very apparent, but a near-the-wood feel is also present. Maintenance is easy; the surfaces need only dusting. Though waxing won't hurt, it isn't needed. The Waterlox finish is resistant to alcohol, stains, and water; any scratches that may occur can be rubbed out and touched up with additional Waterlox.

Pine is soft wood; therefore, it is best to avoid dropping hard objects on the table surfaces. Especially avoid the parts of the table where the surface is almost all end grain.

37.
Bob Ayers' Ducks Unlimited Table

The *Ducks Unlimited* table (Illus. 37-1) is unlike any table you've ever seen. While I'm certainly not advocating that you reproduce it exactly, it does make a wonderful cocktail table for displaying your treasures. Bob Ayers originally made the pieces for charity auctions which raised money for the *Ducks Unlimited* conservation organization. Ayers claims he's not a woodworker, so he has the basic table built for him by another builder, and then he adds his wildlife carvings to the table.

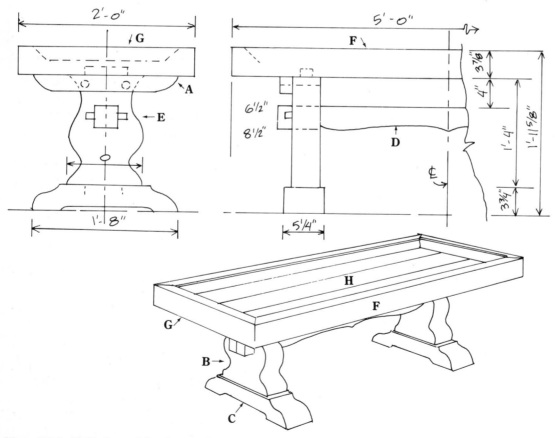

Illus. 37-1. Full-view, side-view and end-view drawings of Bob Ayers' Ducks Un-limited table. Also see page E of the color section and the following page for the parts list.

Parts List for the Ducks Unlimited Table

Label	Part	Quantity	Thickness	Width	Length
A	Top	2	³/₄″	³/₄″	14″
B	Upright	2	3³/₄″	10″	16″
C	Base	2	5¹/₄″	3³/₄″	20″
D	Cross-Brace	1	2″	3³/₄″	47″
E	Tenon Locks	2	³/₄″	³/₄″	4″
F	Long Side Pieces	2	3⅞″	3⅞″	60″
G	Short End Pieces	2	3⅞″	3⅞″	24″
H	Bottom	1	³/₄″	20″	56″

As you study the parts list, you'll see that working with materials this big requires strong tools, a strong builder, and lots of patience.

The outer measurements of the tabletop are 24″ x 60″. The top is made of mitred 4 x 4's which are actually a pair of oak 2 x 4's glued up to form a single piece 3⅞″ x 3⅞″ (Illus. 37-2–37-4). There's a deep tray, the bottom of which is glued-up ³/₄″ oak. Making the mitred frame is basically like making a big, heavy picture frame. As Illus. 37-5 indicates, the mitres are held together with Tite-Joint Fasteners®. I would add two or three rows of biscuits to both align and strengthen this joint. In fact, it seems to me that biscuit-joining the mitres might be both as productive and less expensive than using Tite Joint Fasteners.

There's a rabbet around the inside bottom edge in which the oak bottom rides; you'll do better to cut this rabbet in rather than try to build it in by gluing a smaller piece to the inside. The entire outside of the frame is quarter-rounded with a large radius round-over bit.

The overall height of the table is 18³/₄″, which leaves ¹/₄″ for furniture feet.

The base looks pretty much like the base of a rustic trestle table (Illus. 37-6). All of its components are massive. The feet are 20″ wide, 3³/₄″ high, and 5¹/₄″ thick. The legs are 12″ high, 10″ wide, and 3³/₄″ thick. The trestle piece is positioned dead center on the legs and projects 2″ through each leg. The legs are built 47″ apart, as measured from outside to outside.

When the table is brought to Bob Ayers by the

Illus. 37-2. Underside of the tabletop standing on edge on the table's base.

Illus. 37-3. The top before carving.

Illus. 37-4. The top after carving. Note that the inserts are set in place.

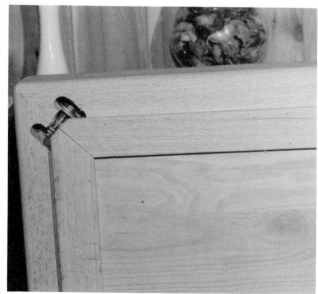

Illus. 37-5. A close-up of the fastener that Ayers' builder used to keep the mitres tight.

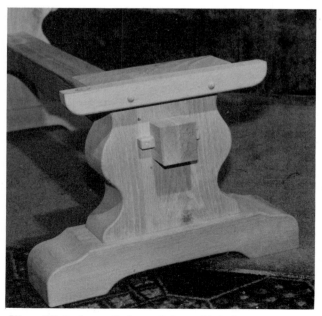

Illus. 37-6. An end view of the table's base.

woodworker who made it, he routs a ¼″ deep by ½″ rabbet, which is a channel for the glass "top" which will be dropped in at the very end of the project. Then he carves out the bottom and carves at an angle into the sides. Some of us might be tempted to cut all four sides at a taper before mitring them; Ayers cuts away his stock so quickly with his hand gouges that tapering the sides would almost seem a wasted effort. The object is to work quickly and to rough-in the shape for the top in the inside edge of the top's outer board. With gouges, waste away approximately half of the sides, on the diagonal. The rougher the better. The total time for this roughing step on the sides and bottom of the display area is around two hours.

Cut a ¾″ x ¾″ rabbet around the inside of the bottom; either square corners with a chisel or round over the corners of the piece you glued up so the insert works well. Use battens to hold the insert in place so that it will be able to "float."

The uprights, bases, and cross-brace can be shaped as desired. Since the cross-brace is not visible, it can be straight. An area of material about 10″ wide and ½″ high must be removed from the bottom-center of the base, to shape the feet. Another option is to use commercial plastic or metal furniture feet.

Ayers carves animals or fish for the inside. He places them inside with an old inoperable rifle or shotgun. After experimenting with the positions and painting and staining the carvings and the table, he dowels the individual carvings in place and then adds some straw flowers to complete the scene. I'll build my table with a three-dimensional representation of my business card logo in it instead of a gun. Instead of the carved animals, there will be some interesting antique tools and, perhaps, some very fine, very curly wood shavings.

Metric Equivalents

INCHES TO MILLIMETRES AND CENTIMETRES

MM—millimetres   CM—centimetres

Inches	MM	CM	Inches	CM	Inches	CM
⅛	3	0.3	9	22.9	30	76.2
¼	6	0.6	10	25.4	31	78.7
⅜	10	1.0	11	27.9	32	81.3
½	13	1.3	12	30.5	33	83.8
⅝	16	1.6	13	33.0	34	86.4
¾	19	1.9	14	35.6	35	88.9
⅞	22	2.2	15	38.1	36	91.4
1	25	2.5	16	40.6	37	94.0
1¼	32	3.2	17	43.2	38	96.5
1½	38	3.8	18	45.7	39	99.1
1¾	44	4.4	19	48.3	40	101.6
2	51	5.1	20	50.8	41	104.1
2½	64	6.4	21	53.3	42	106.7
2	76	7.6	22	55.9	43	109.2
3½	89	8.9	23	58.4	44	111.8
4	102	10.2	24	61.0	45	114.3
4½	114	11.4	25	63.5	46	116.8
5	127	12.7	26	66.0	47	119.4
6	152	15.2	27	68.6	48	121.9
7	178	17.8	28	71.1	49	124.5
8	203	20.3	29	73.7	50	127.0

Index